GAMES THAT DRIVE CHANGE

OTHER TRAINING GAMES BOOKS BY TRAINING McGRAW-HILL:

K. Jones, *Imaginative Events for Training,* 1993

J. J. Kirk & L. D. Kirk, *Training Games for Career Development,* 1994

G. Kroehnert, *100 Training Games,* 1991

C. Nilson, *Team Games for Trainers,* 1993

E. E. Scannell & J. W. Newstrom, *Games Trainers Play,* 1980

E. E. Scannell & J. W. Newstrom, *More Games Trainers Play,* 1983

E. E. Scannell & J. W. Newstrom, *Still More Games Trainers Play,* 1991

E. E. Scannell & J. W. Newstrom, *Even More Games Trainers Play,* 1994

E. E. Scannell & J. W. Newstrom, *The Complete Games Trainers Play,* 1995

GAMES THAT DRIVE CHANGE

Carolyn Nilson

McGraw-Hill, Inc.

New York San Francisco Washington, D.C. Auckland Bogotá
Caracas Lisbon London Madrid Mexico City
Milan Montreal New Delhi San Juan
Singapore Sydney Tokyo Toronto

Library of Congress Cataloging-in-Publication Data

Nilson, Carolyn
    Games that drive change / Carolyn Nilson.
        p.   cm.
    Includes index.
    ISBN 0-07-046589-4 (pbk.)
    1. Organizational change—Management.   2. Communication in
organizations.   I. Title.
    HD58.8.N56   1995
    658.4'06—dc20   95-17015
                                                                              CIP

1 2 3 4 5 6 7 8 9 0   MAL/MAL   9 0 0 9 8 7 6 5

ISBN 0-07-046589-4

The sponsoring editor for this book was James H.
Bessent, Jr., the editing supervisor was Stephen M.
Smith, and the production supervisor was Pamela A.
Pelton.

Printed and bound by Malloy Lithographers, Inc.

DEDICATION

To Noel--
The organization man in the gray flannel suit
who re-engineered himself into a splendid wizard--
my change driver and my love.

ACKNOWLEDGMENTS

To my special family and friends
who inspired some of the graphics in this book--
a great big thank you!

Sari Audette, page 103,
Joe Carotenuti, page 223,
Donna and Jack Colley, page 12,
Lisa Dockendorff, pages 99 and 247,
Adrienne and Bert Holtje, page 155,
Rob Jasmin, page 223,
Eric Nilson, page 169,
Noel Nilson, pages 25, 47, and 157,
Ryan Salame, page 99,
Amy Van Sickle, page 141,
and Doug Smith, page 89.

CONTENTS

SECTION 2: GAMES FOR INTEGRATED SYSTEMS

SECTION 3: GAMES FOR COMMUNICATION

SECTION 4: GAMES FOR ALIGNMENT

SECTION 5: GAMES FOR CONTINUOUS LEARNING

SECTION 6: GAMES FOR JUST IN TIME TRAINING

INDEX

INTRODUCTION

GAMES THAT DRIVE CHANGE is a book of short activities which help people through workplace change. Each activity is separate from the others in the book and is designed to accomplish a narrow objective. Each "game" embodies a principle of play and is meant to lead an individual or group forward into change. The book as a whole is most effectively used as a ready reference book for those who are responsible for managing change and for helping employees successfully through organizational and personal change. The term "game" is used generically to encompass all activities in the book.

A NEW VIEW OF CHANGE

People generally agree that today's change is different from yesterday's change. That is, today's change is not necessarily connected to the past, nor is it predictive of the future. Today's change is discontinuous, requiring, above all else, a flexibility of response. No single predictable, planned approach to change management seems to work. The past is no longer "prologue to the future;" there seem to be very few cyclical trends or linear progressions. The business world within our grasp is indeed a brave new world, demanding risk taking, continuous learning, a new view of information and communication, and a generally creative approach to problem solving. Change today is mostly characterized by disconnects to the past.

1

CHANGE AS PART OF THE BIG PICTURE

Past habits of planning for change and planning one's way through it simply won't work, but this doesn't mean that one's entire business experience has contained no lessons in it. Change must be recognized as a process, not an event, and one's skills and understandings in shaping and implementing process-es must be grounded in past learning from work. Viable organizations don't get that way simply by surviving another quarter; they are created by well-tuned employees at all levels who think and act creatively in response to change's impact on working.

Dramatic, far-reaching changes are occurring at more rapid speed than we have ever experienced before, requiring an arsenal of response tools both at group and organization levels and at individual and personal levels. This book is one such tool.

GAMES AND CHANGE

The activities, exercises, energizers, aha! experiences, illustrations, metaphors, and games in *GAMES THAT DRIVE CHANGE* are each designed to bring the participant to the brink of learning something important about managing the process of change. Games can help to get the creative juices flowing, they can create an atmosphere of playfulness and of thinking on a different plane than people are used to thinking.   Games can add joy to work;

they can help to build trust. They can help people see different "sides" of each other; they can foster communication in new ways. They can be vehicles for action in new directions. A game can facilitate the serious business of clarifying a new principle or making a new procedure easier to understand and adopt. Games are about *dealing* with change and taking charge of it.

Observers to the business scene today warn against the inertia that tends to keep organizations operating according to old ways of doing things. Games can help to challenge that inertia. Personnel and financial resources are being defined differently today: new contractual arrangements, new definitions of worker, new bottom-line goals, new roles for suppliers, and expanded views of customers are all over today's workplaces. Games can help people relate to these new ways of looking at the web of work. Games can make it easier to feel what it's like to approach a situation from a different point of view; games can foster understanding at the gut level when all attempts at a rational approach seem to fail.

Many comments on the state of business today focus on information, communication, and language as products of change and as tools for creating change. This book addresses some of the special concerns associated with generation and application of information; many game-playing skills involving information are illustrated and used in exercises in *GAMES THAT DRIVE*

CHANGE.

Puns, double-meanings, stories, parables, poetry, and acronyms are a few of the ways in which we use or manipulate language to foster understanding. As adults, we have learned to play with words and letters; we have learned innuendo, use of silence, and body language to supplement dialogue. We have learned how to turn tiny electrical impulses bounced off satellites into meaning. Tricks and games with language abound in our business culture today.

Games can fulfill the function of distancing as well as approaching. A metaphor, for example, can be a very effective, powerful, and fast avenue to understanding. On the other hand, the "un-realness" of a game can help a person achieve some distance from a tough problem, and, in the process of playing by the game rules, that person can begin to objectify the problem and more comfortably set about finding its solution. Truth and hard reality can present themselves as overwhelming monsters; sometimes seeing reality through the parameters and filters of a game can increase a person's comfort level at dealing with reality-induced change that faces so many of us at work.

Change makers and change managers must choose games carefully. Used at the right time with the right person, a game can deliver one to the brink of discovery. The following checklist can help you select the right game:

CHECKLIST FOR CHANGE AGENTS

☐ 1. Carefully plan for on-the-job learning; then choose a game that supports, illustrates, or illuminates some part of the plan.

☐ 2. Be sure that you know how to play the game you've chosen; run through it to see if you'll need to modify its contents or procedures and to check it for timing in your situation.

☐ 3. Review the game for potential trouble spots. Be prepared to know how you will handle doubters, obstructionists, and showoffs. Be prepared to modify exercises that don't turn out the way you thought they would.

☐ 4. Be flexible in your presentation or facilitation of the game. Realize that everyone learns at a different rate, and some people are more "natural" than others at playing games. Assemble notes to yourself ahead of time that suggest alternative facilitation techniques in case you need them. Games in this book are designed to be clear in their procedures and narrow in objectives so that use and adaptation are maximized for a wide variety of change agents. Make notes in the margins.

☐ 5. Never play a game just to see who wins and who loses. *GAMES THAT DRIVE CHANGE* are activities that support learning. Stay focused on learning.

HOW THIS BOOK IS ORGANIZED

There are 100 games in this book. Many of these games are enhanced by graphic aids and participant handouts; these checklists, illustrations, and other items may be freely copied and distributed in your organization.

Each game is presented in a similar format to make the book easier to use as a valuable reference document. Each game listing includes these features: objective, procedure, discussion, materials, approximate time required to complete it, and a boxed area near the bottom of the listing containing tips or background information for dealing with change through this particular game. Each game is identified as belonging to one of six key areas of change management. Games are listed in alphabetical order by title within each of the six areas.

Games can also be accessed according to their conceptual content. Readers are encouraged to use the book's INDEX for an alphabetical listing of conceptual material. The games can be used in any order, according to the objectives. Users are advised to browse through the book and use any appropriate pages. The six key areas of change management are:

- **PROCESS RE-DESIGN**
- **ALIGNMENT**
- **INTEGRATED SYSTEMS**
- **CONTINUOUS LEARNING**
- **COMMUNICATION**
- **JUST IN TIME TRAINING**

SECTION 1:
GAMES FOR PROCESS RE-DESIGN

GAMES FOR PROCESS RE-DESIGN
Section Overview

The challenge of driving change, of *managing* organizations through change, begins with the ability to shift one's perspective from job details to job processes. The real edge in management through change is in process management. For too long, management "science" has focused on numbers: "Just gimme the numbers." Numbers were the goals to be reached, and once having gotten there, success was guaranteed.

But today, things are different. Information technology has speeded up and broadened accessibility to numbers as well as enabled the proliferation of other details of business decision making, so that having "the numbers" just isn't the challenge it used to be. Many people other than managers already have "the numbers" and other business details. Time-to-numbers has dramatically changed, causing upheaval in the nature of management. Real management mettle today is tested by the new and complicated processes by which the numbers are disseminated and possessed. By whom? For whom? To whom? When? And how? These are all critical questions that lead managers into the complex area of designing and managing processes. People who can drive processes can drive change. Use these **GAMES FOR PROCESS RE-DESIGN** to "think process."

1. BEAT THE CLOCK
2. BEGIN AT THE END
3. BLOOD, SWEAT, AND TEARS
4. CADENCE
5. CONQUISTADOR OR COLONIST?
6. A CUSTOMER'S NIGHTMARE
7. THE DEVIL YOU KNOW
8. DISENGAGE THE AUTOPILOT
9. FIND THE PAIN
10. FLY SOUTH
11. HOUSEPLANTS
12. INCUMBENCY CURSE
13. KALEIDOSCOPE
14. MOBILE
15. ORGANIZATIONAL MAPPING
16. REINVENTING YOURSELF
17. SO, WHAT'S THE QUESTION?
18. 10% VS. 90%
19. THIS IS ALL I KNOW
20. TOUGH LOVE
21. 20/20

1. BEAT THE CLOCK

from Section 1, GAMES FOR PROCESS RE-DESIGN

OBJECTIVES: To use the principles of motivation from the popular game Beat the Clock in order to make the point that rewards and punishments need to be re-designed to manage change.

To get people thinking differently about specific elements in the compensation system.

PROCEDURE: Use this game in a small group or work team to help members think creatively about options in the re-design of the parts of the compensation system. Choose one small part at a time, such as the salary review process. After completing the re-design of this part, choose another part and repeat the Beat the Clock game to re-set the group's thinking.

Write the "Family Night" advertisement on a flipchart to use in discussion of the Beat the Clock principle of reward, punishment, and motivation: If you arrive:

by 5:00 p.m. your dinner costs	$5.00
by 5:15 p.m............................	$5.15
by 5:30 p.m............................	$5.30

after 6:00 p.m., dinner is regular price, $9.95. Refer back to the restaurant as you need to during your process re-design.

Substitute your own deadlines and rewards from the process of human resources development (HRD) which you've chosen, for example, salary review. Be sure to design into your "game" the rewards of less stress, better relationships, recognition for contribution, increased power, more money, etc. Here's an example of how you might begin:

If reviews of you have been completed by:	You qualify for salary consideration at level:	
customers	IV	(highest)
suppliers	III	
entire department	II	
at least 3 peers	I	
supervisor only	current level	

11

Keep the process of figuring out rewards and punishments going according to the game principles of Beat the Clock.

DISCUSSION: Tell the group about the Beat the Clock game played by a local restaurant as part of its Thursday night "family night" promotion. You'll be surprised at how quickly people move into a planning mode and come up with new ideas as they mentally stretch into the requirements of the new process. Keep the design process going as long as it is productive.

Thanks to Pat and Glenna McCoy for this idea. Here's a copy of the "Beat the Clock" nightly specials from their restaurant, **Mighty Potato,** 826 21st Street, Lewiston, Idaho, telephone (208) 743-SPUD.

Beat the Clock

From 5:00 to 7:00 p.m.   Reg. $8.95 Meal

EXAMPLE
Come in at 5:00 p.m. - Dinner is $5.00
Come in at 5:15 p.m. - Dinner is $5.25
Come in at 5:30 p.m. - Dinner is $5.50

Dinner increases 25¢ each 15 minutes until 7:00 p.m.

Dinner includes: Entree, baked potato or fries, homemade soup or salad, bread & butter and ice cream.

MIGHTY POTATO

Beat the Clock specials reprinted with permission of Pat McCoy.

Taking charge of change often means making drastic changes in the rewards and punishments that affect compensation, benefits, bonuses, and perks of employment. Making change in the process of motivating people to do good work is often the first task that process re-engineers tackle. Look for changes from control to alliance, from exclusive leadership to interactive facilitation. This game is a good vehicle for quickly helping people understand the new value system inherent in the process you have chosen to re-design.

MATERIALS: Flipchart and markers.

TIME REQUIRED: 30 minutes - 2 hours.

2. BEGIN AT THE END
from Section 1, GAMES FOR PROCESS RE-DESIGN

OBJECTIVE: To engage a group of planners in a "futuring exercise."

PROCEDURE: Several days prior to your team or group planning session, distribute an agenda containing the broad categories of processes that must be re-designed in your organization. Some of these categories might include: allocation of time, promotion and retention, quality inspection of product, measurement of productivity, defining the company's mission, generating orders, pulling stock, follow-up to complaints, etc.

Use paper, not e-mail, and suggest that group members bring the agenda with them to the upcoming meeting.

Use this exercise as an "ice breaker" at the beginning of the group planning session. As the planning session begins, instruct group members to have their agendas in front of them for reference.

Now tell them that in today's session they will respond to the statement, "*I am personally most proud of the fact that we achieved....*" Instruct participants to think of themselves in a future time (e.g., 3 years; 6 months; etc.) looking back on the results of their planning today. Ask each person in turn to refer to item #1 on the agenda and respond. Then go on to item #2 on the agenda, and again respond in similar fashion, from the future point of view. Repeat the exercise around the group until all agenda items have been covered.

DISCUSSION: During discussion, group members will take various risks at overestimating and overbudgeting, and engage in various kinds of "outrageous" thinking. This should be encouraged, and will probably be not so outrageous but in the realm of possibility, because you have attached the modifier "I am personally most proud...." People, even in futuring exercises, will build on what they know personally, and so will imbue their answers with some thread of possibility.

As a facilitator for this kind of futuring discussion, your job is to support the risk takers. You can do this by commenting on the worth or value to the company in their past contributions, and you can help people name or identify their own stumbling blocks to getting to that articulated future state. You can be sensitive to the fact that each person in the planning group will be at a different stage of acceptance of change, and that each will be watching and sensing how others are supported during the futuring exercise. Futuring can help otherwise reticent people to speak up with good ideas. Allow plenty of time for interaction between group members so that each can validate the other in various ways during discussion.

Follow up the futuring session with business planning to achieve the desired future states articulated at this meeting.

This exercise is a variation of the old training "warhorse" exercise generally called "Time Capsule." Futuring, by any HRD vehicle, is an exercise that is very useful in getting people to think creatively. It is appealing in dealing with process re-design because it is grounded in past successes. Done the way this exercise suggests, it also has the added interest of helping to empower individual change makers.

MATERIALS: Meeting agendas, paper, pencils; flipchart and
                  markers or blackboard and chalk.

TIME REQUIRED: 15 minutes - 2 hours.

3. BLOOD, SWEAT, AND TEARS

from Section 1, GAMES FOR PROCESS RE-DESIGN

OBJECTIVE: To encourage people to think beyond a narrow definition of re-engineering as they begin their re-design of processes. To remind them that both the scientific approach and the emotional approach are components of a successful re-engineering effort.

PROCEDURE: Reproduce a copy of Winston Churchill's famous World War II speech (p. 17) for each employee to post at his or her workstation as a reminder that their re-engineering efforts must be defined carefully, with attention to organizational and business issues as well as to personal and emotional issues.

Distribute this poster widely, with various cover memos regarding meetings or reports due, throughout the organization as you begin your process re-design. Never lose sight of the human elements of processes.

Distribute articles, models, and opinion pieces that can broaden perspectives about process design to your employees prior to key meetings. Don't rush through the early stages; take the time for people to form ideas. Get the message across early that this is a creative endeavor, not one that is just an exercise in tweaking a few numbers.

DISCUSSION: As you begin to define which processes need attention and why, encourage the broadest possible exposure to re-engineering's full dimensions. One way to do this is through circulation of magazine articles about failures and pitfalls of re-engineering poorly defined; another is through reprints of excerpts from books in anthropology, psychology, or history which take a human systems view of change and progress. Engage people in discussions which can lead to their ownership of the re-design effort; encourage individual inventiveness.

Information Week (Manhasset, NY) magazine, for example, reported that a study by the Arthur D. Little, Inc., consulting firm found that only 16% of executives were satisfied with re-engineering efforts, and that a full 68% said that their re-engineering projects had unintended poor side effects (June 20, 1994, p.52).

Twentieth-century British historian Arnold Toynbee traces a civilization's downward spiral to dependency and bondage through selfishness, complacency, and apathy (**A Study of History**, New York: Oxford University Press, 1972). Fellow historians Will and Ariel Durant urge thoughtful persons throughout changing times to pay attention to the positive and the negative manifestations of various "character elements," such as the positive wonder and the negative doubt, the positive resolution and the negative acceptance, the positive anger and the negative fear (**The Lessons of History**, New York: Simon and Schuster, 1968, p.33).

Martin Luther King, Jr.'s famous "I Have a Dream" speech before the Lincoln Memorial on August 28, 1963 can provide new inspiration to a generation of process re-designers who come after King. In addition to his oft-quoted "I have a dream..." sentences, this speech contains other well-crafted words and aspirations of a change-maker. Consider these:

"We refuse to believe that there are insufficient funds in the great vaults of opportunity of this nation." And this, "As we walk, we must make the pledge that we shall always march ahead." (**I Have a Dream**, edited by J.M. Washington, San Francisco: HarperSanFrancisco, 1992, pp.102f.)

Much has been made of the definition of re-engineering. The sharpen-your-pencil-green-eyeshade-analytical "re-engineer" stereotype frequently gets organizations into trouble. As people begin efforts to make their organizations better, they need reminders to consider not only the sweat and the labor of the enterprise, but also the uniquely human aspects of the organization-- the feelings, beliefs, and values which keep people wanting to give their best at work.

MATERIALS: Various handouts prior to initial meetings.

TIME REQUIRED: 10 - 60 minutes for research, copying, and
                          distribution.

"*I would say to the House, as I said to those who have joined this Government,*

'I have nothing to offer but blood, toil, tears and sweat'."

Winston Churchill,
House of Commons, 13 May 1940

from The Oxford Dictionary of Quotations, 3rd Edition, Oxford University Press, 1980, p.149.

4. CADENCE

from Section 1, GAMES FOR PROCESS RE-DESIGN

OBJECTIVE: To experience a different way of thinking, that is, "changed thinking," by using music and not words as the change driver.

PROCEDURE: Enlist the help of a group member or other employee who can play an instrument, preferably an instrument on which chords can be played (for example, a guitar, banjo, dulcimer, autoharp, accordion, electronic keyboard). This exercise is especially appropriate for use at an off-site visioning or re-engineering conference.

At any time during a planning session for process re-design, break for a music lesson in cadence, relying on the performing ability of your guest musician. Ask the musician to play a familiar short song all the way through. (A good attention-getter right after lunch or coffee break.)

After defining what musical cadence means (see below) ask the musician to play the song again, but at cadence places, play a different chord from that which is expected. Use songs that are familiar to the group, so that they can feel how strange it feels at a gut level when the unfamiliar chord disturbs the expected cadence. An example of two contrasting cadences is provided on page 21.

Use this non-verbal "game" to illustrate that process re-design might feel like the strange chord, but, in fact, building new music with the same old notes is very much like what re-design of processes is all about.

DISCUSSION: Explain to the group that a cadence is the natural progression of music in chords to an anticipated end, or closure at the end of a musical phrase. Cadence is a cultural phenomenon, a learned expectation. That is, European classical music has one kind of expectation for musical closure; Indian music or Chinese music have other kinds of cadences; American rock and roll or "Country Music" have their own; Irish folk music has its special kinds of cadences.

19

A skillful musician can demonstrate several typical, culturally learned cadences. Folk music and patriotic songs work well.

Your task as facilitator or leader of the process re-design is to help people feel the comfort of a familiar cadence and then be willing to engage in changes to the music in order to go with the direction of a new, perhaps strange, cadence. Through music, many people can begin to understand at a visceral, emotional level just how it feels to experience change.

Use people's experience of the cadence change to encourage them to talk about their feelings about change in general and organizational change in particular. Use the powerful metaphor of the cadence to lead planners into re-design of processes that will help create a new culture in your organization.

Much has been written about how "attitude" problems get in the way of participation in and commitment to change. Culturally learned self-preservation behaviors at work seem to be the comfortable "cadence." Use this game to help attitudes to change.

MATERIALS: A musician and some simple songs to illustrate cadences.

TIME REQUIRED: 10 - 20 minutes.

CADENCE

1

Twin-kle, twin-kle, lit - tle star, How I won-der what you are.

2

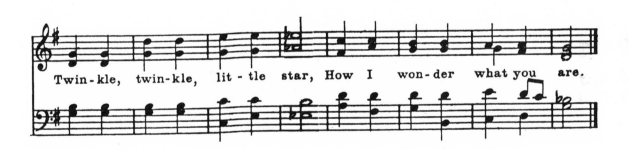

Twin-kle, twin-kle, lit - tle star, How I won-der what you are.

5. CONQUISTADOR OR COLONIST?

from Section 1, GAMES FOR PROCESS RE-DESIGN

OBJECTIVES: To play a simple "column A or column B?" identifying game as an icebreaker or energizer at a group session on process re-design.

To use the metaphor of conquistador and colonist to illustrate two contrasting attitudes about how current processes are working in an organization.

PROCEDURE: As group members assemble, give each a CONQUISTADOR OR COLONIST? handout like the one on page 25.

When you are ready to begin, tell the group that this will be a short "test" in placing some items in the correct column. Instruct them to place each item that you will read in either the column CONQUISTADOR or the column COLONIST, according to the way each sees it. (There is no right or wrong-- you are simply trying to assess the current situation and get individuals to make a commitment as to how they see things.)

Suggest to the group that, according to history, the CONQUISTADOR came to the new world to plunder and take something away from it, while the COLONIST came to the new world to build. The challenge of the "test" for the group is to place a current process happening in the organization in either the taking away column or the building column. CONQUISTADOR = destruction, COLONIST = construction.

Here is the list. Add any more processes you can think of-- customize the list for your own situation. Read them one by one, allowing a few seconds of thinking and writing time. Wait until all have finished each item before going on to the next one.

<u>list of processes</u>
- the way top managers lead
- internal communication
- customer service
- flow of paper
- flow of work
- continuing education and training
- working in teams
- financial rewards for doing work
- prospecting for sales
- developing budgets

DISCUSSION: How people see the processes at work affecting their lives and the health of the company matters. In this exercise, expect some similarity of response as well as some responses that are hard to categorize and that differ greatly.

Be prepared to delve into people's reasons for choosing one column over the other; use this exercise to begin a dialogue about the need to change destructive processes or parts of processes, and to support the processes or parts of processes that contribute to constructive growth.

Simple exercises like this one can be effectively used as a springboard for deeper analysis. At the deeper level, focus on complexity of process, characteristics of commitment required, range and cost of resources needed, level and types of expertise demanded, spinoffs anticipated, etc. Keep trying to probe responses to get at the critical elements involved in re-design. Go for changes that add value.

MATERIALS: CONQUISTADOR OR COLONIST? (page 25) handout for each person in the group.

TIME REQUIRED: 15 minutes; longer if it leads to dialogue.

CONQUISTADOR OR COLONIST?

CONQUISTADOR?   # COLONIST?

1.

2.

3.

4.

5.

6.

7.

8.

9.

10.

25

6. A CUSTOMER'S NIGHTMARE

from Section 1, GAMES FOR PROCESS REDESIGN

OBJECTIVE: To focus on a "broken" process through a classic imagining exercise.

PROCEDURE: Tell your group to imagine that they are customers. That is, each person imagines that he or she is *his or her own customer*. If people don't have a direct customer, suggest that each identify an internal customer, one next in line to receive a person's service or product.

Be sure that each person has identified a specific customer, attaching a name to that customer, if possible, so that the customer becomes a real human being in the person's mind. Take time to be sure that each has identified a customer. Help those who can't imagine a customer to find one-- the group is usually good at supplying suggestions.

Now tell your group to imagine that customer's worst nightmare-- misinformation, sloppy communication, deadline long gone, overruns, poor quality, lies, cheating, political maneuvering, etc. Instruct each person to be as specific as possible, that is, what specifically is his or her customer's worst nightmare? Suggest that they write it down on a piece of paper, so it stares them in the face for the rest of this process re-design meeting.

DISCUSSION: Encourage group discussion about each nightmare. Search for solutions to the failed process(es) identified during this "nightmare" exercise. Work in brainstorming fashion, allowing all comments and giving them equal weight.

This type of exercise is known as a "working backward" form of problem solving. Adding the dimension of imagination to it helps to encourage free-flowing responses.

MATERIALS: Paper and pencils.

TIME REQUIRED: 20 minutes - 1 hour.

7. THE DEVIL YOU KNOW

from Section 1, GAMES FOR PROCESS RE-DESIGN

OBJECTIVE:
To spell out the "devils you know" that are working hard and persistently to create obstacles to organizational change.

PROCEDURE:
Use this exercise as an energizer during a planning session.

Get the group's attention by showing the "devil" overhead transparency (page 31). Use it to help them identify the processes, procedures, relationships, etc., that need to be changed. This exercise is especially useful at the beginning of process re-design or in the early stages of implementation of change. Use it to get people to identify the problems.

It can also be useful as a refresher exercise to make a work group stop and re-think a direction that doesn't seem to be yielding the hoped-for results.

DISCUSSION:
The "devil you know" is always more familiar and more comfortable than the "devil you don't know." Unfortunately, the devil you don't know is often in your midst before the devil you know has gone. That's the problem with change.

The trick in this exercise is to see problems objectively-- to take yourself outside of the comfort of "but this is the way we've always done things." Try to get the group to identify exactly what the problems are with doing things the same old way; try to get them to identify what the real "rules of the game" are.

Two popular authors have dealt with this issue in current publications. Review either or both of them for more in-depth consideration. These references are: P. Pritchett, PhD, **Culture Shift**, Dallas: Pritchett Publishing Co., 1993; and P. Scott-Morgan, **The Unwritten Rules of the Game**, New York: McGraw-Hill, Inc., 1994.

MATERIALS:
THE DEVIL YOU KNOW! overhead transparency (page 31).

TIME REQUIRED: 10 minutes - 2 hours.

THE DEVIL YOU KNOW!

8. DISENGAGE THE AUTOPILOT

from Section 1, GAMES FOR PROCESS RE-DESIGN

OBJECTIVE:
To use a set of mini-case studies to suggest approaches that your organization can take to change.

PROCEDURE:
Use the metaphor of "disengaging the autopilot" to help your planning teams think of stopping the automatic responses and systems that have been "flying blind" on autopilot.

This exercise can be used as a group or team exercise, or it can be used as self-study exercise done individually at one's desk.

For several weeks prior to doing this exercise, search the popular business press, general news magazines, airline magazines, and other general-audience current periodicals for write-ups of companies that truly shook things up-- "disengaged their autopilots" and took control of their organizational change. Look in magazines such as **Newsweek**, **Time**, **Business Week**, **Forbes**, **Forbes ASAP**, **Information Week**, **Fortune**, **Training**, and other magazines readily available. Photocopy key articles, with their appropriate credit lines-- title, author, pages, issue date-- or summarize the article yourself, and distribute each article under a cover page that says "DISENGAGE THE AUTOPILOT." Keep the sources general, so that readers can understand in plain English what happened.

Use a cover sheet like the one suggested on page 35. Fill in the blank regarding which company the article highlights. Staple the cover sheet to the article or summary; give people several days to read the article before getting together to discuss the cases. Limit your cases to no more than 3 at one distribution. Encourage everyone to read the same cases.

DISCUSSION:
When you do convene the planning session, facilitate freewheeling discussion about what each company did and how change helped the company achieve success. Natural-

ly, then ask your group what you can adapt from the case studies as you begin to "disengage your own autopilots."

Here are some of the kinds of stories to look for as you go through the magazines:

(1)   Tandy's ambitious retailing project building Computer City and Incredible Universe megastores. The shopping experience will include karaoke booths, gourmet cooking demonstrations and tastings, and other hands-on experiences in various entertainment and appliance sections of the stores. Each Computer City store is expected to require $1 million in initial construction costs and $4 million for start-up inventory.

> *from* Delta Airlines' **Sky** magazine, in a article by Jeffrey Zygmont, "Tandy Takes on Tomorrow," April 1994, pp.60ff.

(2)   Amaco's early re-engineering failures stemmed from "not recognizing the interrelationship between management practices and processes." Amaco's CFO cited, for example, the case of capital budgeting, which seemed like a staff function. Amaco's early mistake was to essentially "go on autopilot" by having staff people re-engineer the capital budgeting process. Success came when line managers were brought into the re-design process and worked on teams with staff people. They made progress when they "disengaged."

> *from* **Information Week**, Special Report by Bruce Caldwell, June 20, 1994, p.60.

The autopilot is the aircraft's control mechanism that maintains a pre-set course. It's always easy to keep going on that pre-set path. Use the autopilot image with actual mini-case studies to spark a creativity that's grounded in reality. The use of case study is a good way for many otherwise reticent employees to begin to imagine what's possible. The extra overlay of the autopilot metaphor can help bring out their inventiveness.

MATERIALS: DISENGAGE THE AUTOPILOT case studies from magazines.

TIME REQUIRED: 15 - 30 minutes reading time; 1 - 2 hours for discussion.

"DISENGAGE THE AUTOPILOT"

COVER SHEET FOR CASE STUDY

_____

company name

source and date of this article:

_____
_____

9. FIND THE PAIN
from Section 1, GAMES FOR PROCESS RE-DESIGN

OBJECTIVE: To reward persons for finding "the pain," that is, the various ways of currently doing things that contribute to the "dis-ease" of the organization. To give whistle-blowers and "crap detectors" visible support when they identify problems. To make an obvious show of recognizing those who honestly and truthfully try to help change processes that contribute to stalemate and business-as-usual.

PROCEDURE: Photocopy the light bulb found on page 39 onto bright colored copy paper. (For example, Strathmore makes a 60 pound offset paper known as "Brite-Hue," available at most office supply stores.) Choose bright gold or yellow paper. Cut out the bulb if you choose.

Keep a large supply of these light bulbs in key places, for example, with team leaders, supervisors, managers, trainers, etc. Estimate at least 10 light bulbs for each person in the organization. Produce more if you need them as the idea catches on.

Instruct each person responsible for leadership (managers, supervisors, etc.) to hand out light bulbs to be posted visibly in a person's office or workstation, as recognition that this person discovered something that can help shed light on the effort at process re-design. Encourage the leader to suggest that the person being recognized identify the bright idea on the stem of the light bulb as a reminder to all who see it.

This game works best within a definite time frame, such as 2 weeks, 1 month, 6 weeks. Give it a time limit to encourage focused thinking. Start the game at a staff or team meeting at which you have a pile of light bulbs ready to be distributed to the good thinkers-- the inventors.

DISCUSSION: This activity can be useful at the beginning to your change efforts, as a visible signal that you intend to congratulate and recognize truthful thinking. Promote this as a "game" and keep it going throughout the organization/company during a concentrated period such as one month. Give plenty of verbal praise to anyone who has been awarded light bulbs. Demonstrate your pleasure at people taking a stand for improvement; show by your obvious support of the risk taker that with their help you intend to rid the organization of those painful things that contribute to organizational dysfunction.

Let your group know that even Thomas Edison didn't get it right the first time: it is said that it took him 9,000 different experiments before he achieved a working light bulb (reported in an article by Michael Michalko, "Bright Ideas," in **Training & Development** magazine, June 1994, p.47). Using the term "9,000 THINGS THAT DIDN'T WORK" on the light bulb itself will help remind your thinkers that innovation is built upon learning from experiments that didn't quite work. The thing that's rewarded is a person's realization that something should be fixed.

Organization development guru and Harvard University professor, Chris Argyris, coined the term "Skilled Incompetence," by which he means the learned behaviors and ways of doing things that prevent organizational learning to occur. Those familiar with Argyris's work will recognize his "double loop" learning model as a way to get out of the skilled incompetence trouble. Peter Senge, "Learning Organization" guru, in many of his writings, acknowledges the influence on his work of Argyris's double loop model. This FIND THE PAIN activity helps address finding that double loop which then can lead to positive organizational change.

For further reading, see any articles by Chris Argyris in recent issues of **Harvard Business Review**, or recent books by Argyris, such as **Knowledge for Action, Barriers to Overcoming Organizational Change**, San Francisco, Jossey-Bass, 1993. See also, Peter Senge's two books: **The Fifth Discipline, The Art & Practice of The Learning Organization**, New York, Doubleday Currency, 1990; or Senge et al., **The Fifth Discipline Fieldbook**, also Doubleday Currency, 1994.

MATERIALS: A supply of paper light bulbs, master found on page 39.

TIME REQUIRED: Several minutes to hand out light bulbs to innovative thinkers.

"9,000 THINGS
THAT DIDN'T WORK"

T.A. Edison (1847-1931)

10. FLY SOUTH

from Section 1, GAMES FOR PROCESS RE-DESIGN

OBJECTIVES: To tell short stories to a group of changemakers in order to help them be innovative in their approach to change. To encourage people to consider re-writing the rules of work. To use the stories to suggest the creation of thinking tools and software programs to help people explore different ways of thinking about simple work and organizational processes.

PROCEDURE: This activity takes its name from the position of birds migrating south from northern locales. The most familiar image is that of geese flying in a "V" formation. The ideas in FLY SOUTH can be expressed through many kinds of stories; for this purpose in this book, the stories begin with a bird story.

Stories here (see page 43) are all adapted from an article, "Changing the Centralized Mind," by Mitchel Resnick, Assistant Professor at the Massachusetts Institute of Technology Media Laboratory, in the July 1994 issue of MIT's **Technology Review**, pp.32ff. Many sources can be tapped for good stories; those from outside of the field of human resources development, TQM, and organization development should be pursued most ardently. Those suggested here are examples.

Read or distribute via electronic mail or paper copy the four stories to your work team or organizational group. Suggest that they read the stories to gain new insight into the world around us. Meet as a group to discuss the insights.

DISCUSSION: These four particular stories show how decentralized and random phenomena or processes can guide progress. They demonstrate that change does not always happen because of planned leadership or central control. These particular stories can be used as background for changes regarding employee empowerment and shared responsibility. These stories can provide analogies to analysis of the "rules" that currently govern your organization.

Principles of behavior and human relationships are often learned better when they can be demonstrated by stories, based on fact, from fields that are seemingly unrelated to one's present concerns. The terminology and the processes of contrasting fields can spark one's creativity; rules of a new field can suddenly shed light on reconstruction of the rules of one's own field. While traditional exposition ("showing and telling") encourages rational response, storytelling encourages creative response. The purpose of a story is not to tell people how to think, but rather to suggest a mental context in which people can expand their thinking in new ways.

MATERIALS: A set of stories for each group member.

TIME REQUIRED: 15 minutes reading and thinking time;
                       additional time for group discussion as needed.

Stories That Challenge Central Leadership

1. FLY SOUTH

Contrary to what people think, most birds flying in "V" formation are not actually following a leader: they are following a simple set of behavioral rules that govern the actions of each member of the flock. The simple rules are: match your velocity to the velocity of the birds around you, and keep a safe distance from the birds on each side of you. The rule is *not* "watch the leader and do what the leader does."

from Mitchel Resnick, "Changing the Centralized Mind," Technology Review, July 1994, pp.32-33.

2. LONG, LONG TRAIL A-WINDING

Anyone who's ever watched a parade of ants marvels at how they blaze their trails. People like to believe that the queen ant somehow dictates where worker ants should go, being the wise and good matriarch that she is. People like to believe that a benevolent leader sends forth her armies to do their best work and to preserve the kingdom (queendom?).

What actually happens is that in ant colonies, it's the interactions between workers that determine the trail patterns-- where business will be done, and where sustenance will be found. In ant life, one of the simple rules is that when you find food, send out a scent. Another simple rule is follow the scent.

from Mitchel Resnick, "Changing the Centralized Mind," Technology Review, July 1994, pp.34-35.

3. TRAFFIC JAM

Mitchel Resnick at MIT created a simulation language called StarLogo which allows users to control the interactions of thousands of graphic images through creation of simple behavioral rules. In one experiment, some of his students created rules about speed limits and radar traps on highways in an attempt to "create" a traffic jam.

To the students' great surprise, the cars did not need the "centralized control" of a radar trap in order for a traffic jam to occur. In fact, what causes most traffic jams is the slowing down of cars who randomly happen to get "too near" one another. When this "too near-ness" happened, it was likely that nearby cars, especially cars that followed, would also slow down thereby creating the traffic

43

jam. The aggregation is not explained by the controlling trigger (central authority), nor by a rational "wave theory." The traffic jam seems to be typically explained by some kind of rule of mutual proximity.

from Mitchel Resnick, "Changing the Centralized Mind," Technology Review, July 1994, pp.36-37, 39.

4. PIT BULLS AND BEARS

In spite of media hype about certain individuals and "institutional" megatrades that control stock buying and selling, what really happened in the pits of stock exchanges is patterns of pricing being determined by millions of interactions around the world.

We'd like to think that our very own broker-- our "Senior Vice President" and his brilliant research team backup-- is the one who controls the best time for buying and selling; our centralized mindset makes us more comfortable relating to authority in matters of money. What really happens is a macro-economic phenomenon of patterning via mass processing-- the arguing, haggling, hustling, buying, and selling being simultaneously done and massively transmitted. The way in which stocks and commodities behave on the charts is the result of massively decentralized parallel actions and massive random interactions.

from Mitchel Resnick, "Changing the Centralized Mind," in Technology Review, July 1994, p.37.

11. HOUSEPLANTS

from Section 1, GAMES FOR PROCESS RE-DESIGN

OBJECTIVE: To spark creativity through an old-fashioned "object lesson"
               using houseplants (office plants). To encourage creative
               or "way out" thinking about process re-design.

PROCEDURE: From the offices of group participants, round up office plants
               such as grape ivy, spider plant, philodendron, yucca, cactus,
               etc. Ask people to bring their plants to a group meeting.

               Line up all of the plants next to each other on a table in front
               of the group. Arrange them so that contrasting plants are
               side by side. Use the "objects," that is, the plants, to make a
               point about organizational design.

               Ask the group to come up and carefully study each plant in
               terms of how it grows-- where new growth originates, effects
               of sunlight or darkness that they observe in the shape of the
               plant, effects of too much or too little watering, evidence of
               the plant's shedding old or used up parts, etc. Suggest that
               each person develop a mental list of each plant's processes
               of life. Suggest that they be aware of contrasts among the
               various plants.

               After the group observes the plants, ask them to be seated
               again. When the group settles down, lead a discussion of
               their observations. Hold up each plant, one by one, as group
               members report their observations. Suggest that as they go
               through this exercise they look for parallels in organization
               design. Use the "objective" study of plants as an analogy for
               study of the organization.

DISCUSSION: The drawing on page 47 illustrates points of discussion.
               Help your group to see that "living systems"-- plants as well
               as organizations-- respond and adapt to environments,
               whether these environmental factors are good or bad. Help
               them to see parallels between the plants and the
               organization. At the end of the meeting, send them back to
               their offices with their plants. They probably will never look at

their plants the same way again, and, who knows, that plant just might become an inspiration for organizational change!

Canadian professor Gareth Morgan has written a fascinating book, **Images of Organization**, Newbury Park, CA: Sage Publications, 1986. In it, he views organizations through the lenses of other entities, such as organizations as machines, as living organisms, as brains, as political systems, as instruments of domination, and others. The table of contents of this book is one of the most interesting of any organizational development book on the market today.

Professor Morgan suggests that use of metaphor implies a way of seeing and of thinking; it is not only a creative writing technique or word game. In this exercise, we use the metaphor of the plants to see and think about organizational environments in a new way. Using the living system metaphor can also be an ever-present challenge to the more typical machine or mechanical metaphor that often pervades thinking about organizations.

Object lessons have been used for decades, maybe even centuries, as a device to help students discover truths about one situation by objectifying the study of a metaphorical situation. "HOUSEPLANTS" is one such lesson.

MATERIALS: Office plants from offices of group members.

TIME REQUIRED: 10 - 20 minutes.

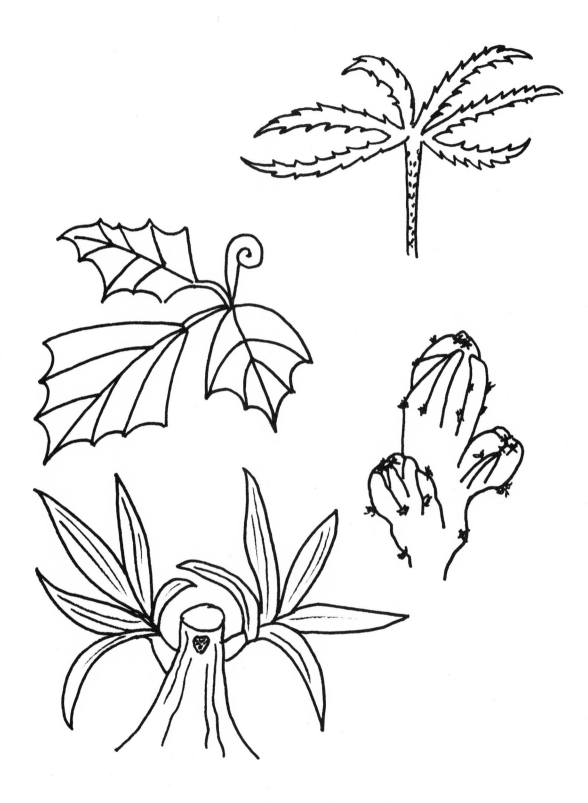

12. INCUMBENCY CURSE
from Section 1, GAMES FOR PROCESS RE-DESIGN

OBJECTIVE: To use techniques and approaches of political analysis to analyze needs for process re-design. To help planners experience the political truth-- the incumbency curse-- that bad times damage the incumbent more than good times help.

PROCEDURE: There are two simple ways to engage change-drivers in process analysis using the approach of political analysis: one is to use newspaper articles about well-known elected officials (local, state, or federal) currently in office , and the other is to use your own company's annual report. Use these documents as the raw material of your "game" study.

Use this exercise as an icebreaker exercise at a staff meeting or team meeting before you focus on your own specific problem of process re-design. Or, use it during a planning retreat or workshop to "shift gears" from one agenda item to another.

Photocopy or obtain enough copies of your "raw materials" for each person to have one set of materials. Hand them out at the beginning of the session to each person. Instruct them to take a few minutes and read the items (if you use an annual report, skip the financial statements pages-- just read the narrative text).

As you listen in silence as they read, you will soon hear chuckles, exclamations of disbelief, howls of incredulity, etc. as readers make it rather clear that they don't believe the good words written in these documents. They are beginning to experience what's known as "the curse of incumbency."

DISCUSSION: Capitalize on this somewhat negative energy to facilitate a short discussion of people's actual experience with the person or the subject of the writing. You'll hear both good and bad. That is, some people are willing to give the person written about the benefit of the doubt, and other people think that the writing is all lies and smoke screens.

49

Your task, after everyone has "vented," is to point out that the political phenomenon of the incumbency curse seems to derive from the public's need to evaluate against an ideal. Incumbent corporate officers, senators, and local mayors all have an uphill battle to keep constituents grounded in reality and not impressionism. Publics of all sorts seem to want peace, harmony, justice, goodness; they elect an ideal. Incumbents (that is, real people) can never win against an ideal.

Try to get your group to realize that change is tough work, and that incumbents are always judged harshly. Those entrusted or empowered to make change almost always have to endure the curse of incumbency. This exercise will help them to identify with and understand better the tough task ahead. Try to get them to realize that cynicism won't help solve the problems, and that clear analysis on their part about how to get rid of the bad stuff will eventually pay off.

If you can't find local writing that seems appropriate, turn to national news magazines or metropolitan newspapers with "Washington News" columns. Two very good examples of "cursed incumbents" are President Bill Clinton and President Nelson Mandela of South Africa. Failures against an ideal in Clinton's ambitious domestic and foreign programs "curse" his solid economic successes, and Mandela's great successes in many domestic areas are constantly being obscured by the public's unrealistic yardstick ideal of the "First 100 Days."

MATERIALS: Reprints of news articles, and/or annual reports.

TIME REQUIRED: 15 - 20 minutes.

13. KALEIDOSCOPE

from Section 1, GAMES FOR PROCESS RE-DESIGN

OBJECTIVE: To use the kaleidoscope as a symbol of re-design.

PROCEDURE: Place kaleidoscopes in public areas during a time that is designated as planning time or re-design time in your company. Keep them there until the design period officially ends and implementation begins. This could be anywhere from a week to several months.

Find interesting texture kaleidoscopes, ones of varying sizes and diameters, ones with unusual glass or stones inside. Place them in areas where people informally gather, such as foyers and lobbies, lounges, lunchrooms, vending machines, copy machines, FAX machines. Place a different one on each cafeteria table as a centerpiece. Make them attractive and accessible so that people randomly pick them up-- kaleidoscopes are hard to resist if they're right there!

Adopt a "change" slogan during the time kaleidoscopes are visible. Post the slogan on electronic bulletin boards, with the morning's news or weather, and on posters and memos. Here are some suggestions: "See In A New Way" "Grab Hold Of Change" "A Different View" "Get Ready To Readjust" "Bright Lights In Your Future."

DISCUSSION: This is a "soft-sell" activity that seeks to create a metaphor for changing the process. Allow it to take its course, gently encouraging people to play with the kaleidoscope as the spirit moves them. The most appropriate dialogue during play is to simply encourage more play by asking rhetorically, "How many different views did you get?" The answer to the question isn't important; you are simply encouraging people to "get their hands around" change. Use that random group experience at some later planning meeting as a powerful device for understanding the possibilities that can result from changing the process.

The value of this playtime will be in how you can work with your people's individual and group memory of the kaleidoscope changes. Memory research over the years has indicated that the more senses (touching, seeing, hearing) are involved, the more vivid the memory will be. The "instrumentalists" also believe that the act of doing things, getting involved in a hands-on way with an object, will help to anchor that act of involvement-- the process-- in memory. With cues from a leader or facilitator at a later date, those vivid memories can be brought to the surface and used as a springboard to understanding the complex business problem at hand.

MATERIALS: A variety of kaleidoscopes and a catchy slogan or two.

TIME REQUIRED: One minute every now and then.

14. MOBILE

from Section 1, GAMES FOR PROCESS RE-DESIGN

OBJECTIVE: To build a mobile representing the balancing of key processes in the design of the "new organization."

PROCEDURE: This can be done as a project within a team or work group, or it can be done at a larger workshop or off-premises planning retreat as a project by small groups working simultaneously.

Assemble heavy paper of various colors, scissors, paper punch, markers, bamboo skewers, and thin string or nylon thread-- in enough quantity for each group to construct a mobile. Give these supplies to the group seated around a table where they will build the mobile.

To save time, use the patterns provided on pages 55, 57, and 59. Enlarge or reduce them on your office copier. Photocopy them onto brightly colored paper or card stock.

To begin mobile building, suggest that all participants examine the shapes to be sure that all people understand what the options are. Have extra blank paper and markers so that additional shapes can be added at the group's discretion.

Give each person or group a copy of the "Process Lists" on page 61. These are some options of processes that must be in balance. Each group is responsible for writing the name of one process on each shape to be placed in the mobile. The trick is to balance the shapes and the processes on them.

Instruct them to simply get started. Set a time limit and wait for the interesting finished products. The goal is to build a balanced mobile.

DISCUSSION: Take some time to display and talk about the finished mobiles. Try to get participants to answer "why these processes need to be in balance" and "what is going to be involved in keeping these processes in balance."

53

Hang the completed mobile(s) in strategic places around the organization.

Much has been made by those studying change in recent years of the need to replace the so-called scientific management articulated by Frederick Winslow Taylor a generation ago with a more dynamic, more mobile view of organizations. This new view is very appropriate when thinking about process change, or process re-design.

An excellent article in **Harvard Business Review**, November-December 1993, explores this issue in depth. See "Managing Change: The Art of Balancing" by Jeanie Daniel Duck, pp. 109-118. Reprints of this article would make a good follow-up to the mobile-building experience.

MATERIALS: Materials for making a mobile (see above description, under Procedure; patterns for making mobile parts, found on pp. 55, 57, and 59; a "Process List" (p. 61) for each participant.

TIME REQUIRED: 30 minutes - 1 hour.

PATTERNS FOR MOBILE PARTS

PATTERNS FOR MOBILE PARTS

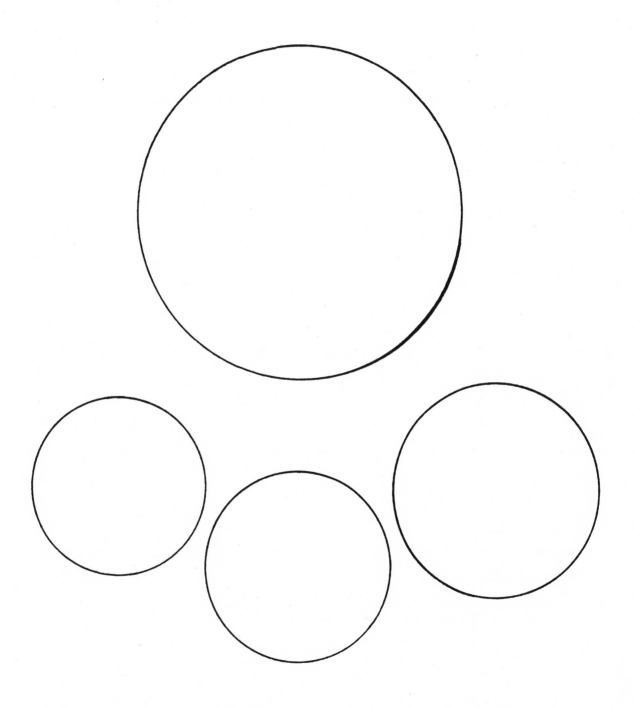

PATTERNS FOR MOBILE PARTS

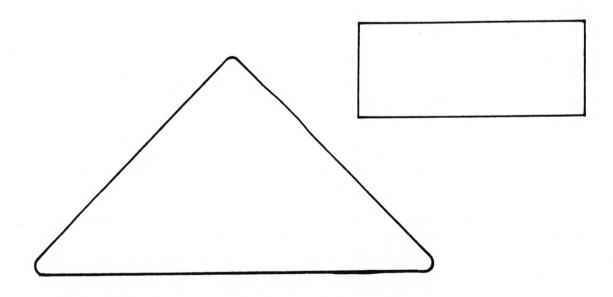

PROCESS LISTS

Note: Five different lists are presented here. Choose any of these processes, or identify your own as you create your mobile. They are included here to spark your imagination!

List 1
managing quality
empowering employees
serving customers
defining vision
providing leadership

List 2
preserving commitment
maintaining momentum
communicating
monitoring work
defining projects
rewarding excellence
solving problems
creating information
learning
providing support

List 3
accounting
investing
researching
designing
engineering
processing data
training
recruiting
allocating resources

List 4
working in teams
eliminating layers
improving productivity
developing skills
sharing information
designing jobs

List 5
speeding
taking risks
staying cool
identifying errors
asking questions
imagining
reflecting
dialoging
fixing
doing
thinking

15. ORGANIZATIONAL MAPPING
from Section 1, GAMES FOR PROCESS RE-DESIGN

OBJECTIVE: To create a strategic process design for a familiar product or service, with the goals of maximum customer (internal or external) satisfaction, optimal cost (just low enough for best quality), and enhanced competitive positioning.

PROCEDURE: This game is best played in a group large enough to break into several smaller work groups of 3 - 5 persons. It is a good activity to do at a planning retreat or workshop.

Break into small groups and assemble each group around a work table. Distribute packs of white and colored index cards to each table. Give each table one pack of white, one pack of blue, one pack of pink, and one pack of yellow cards and several black markers with which to write on the cards.

The task of each table is to work as a process design team and create the best possible process design for an agreed-upon problem product or service. Some ideas are: production of an internal employee newsletter; production, packaging, or assembly of a specific product; providing room service to a guest at a hotel. Choose any specific, limited service or product whose beginning and end can be identified. Give the group about 10 minutes to identify this item. (It should end with a customer-- either within the company or external to it.)

Explain that the index cards will represent "boxes" in a typical flow chart, and that each group's task is to map the organizational processes, in appropriate relationships, that should contribute to this product or service's movement through the company. Markers are available to label each card with the appropriate process or subprocess. Arrows can be drawn on the card to indicate the direction of flow, that is, either up, down, or across.

For example:

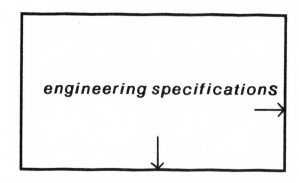

Suggest that each group use white cards for the biggest or highest level process, blue for the next level, pink for the next, and yellow for the lowest level or most detailed subprocess.

Remind the group of the objective of this exercise, that is, to design the best possible process for customer satisfaction, cost, and competitiveness.

DISCUSSION: After the groups have finished their organizational mapping of one process (groups can be working on different processes--anything of the group's choosing), suggest that they walk around the room and see what the other groups have done.

Facilitate a freewheeling discussion around each table.

In process redesign, it is important for work teams to have the occasion to " play at," that is, to experiment with very flexible ways to represent their individual thoughts. Using the unintimidating format of index cards helps to encourage individual contribution to the design effort. The exercise of mapping, or flowcharting, helps people maintain a systems view.

MATERIALS: Four packages of index cards, white plus three colors per table of workers; several markers per table.

TIME REQUIRED: 30 - 60 minutes.

16. REINVENTING YOURSELF

from Section 1, GAMES FOR PROCESS RE-DESIGN

OBJECTIVES: To pause and reconsider why you yourself are doing things the way you are; to then identify better ways of doing those things.

PROCEDURE: Use this brief exercise as a "pause that refreshes" during a meeting or in a discussion that is generally focused on systemic, not personal, change. Use it as an "energizer" during a meeting that seems to be going nowhere.

Distribute cold soft drinks or juice as a symbol of the pause that refreshes, or open a window to emphasize the "fresh air" approach, as you begin this exercise. As soon as each person in the group has experienced the fresh approach (tasted the drink or felt the breeze), tell them that you are going to shift gears from where the meeting left off and that now they will talk about themselves.

Phrase all questions in terms of the individual, and tell them that their responses should use the word "I" in them. Some easy "I" actions are: I think, I believe, I understand, I made, I sent, I put, I wrote. If people are having a hard time expressing answers in "I" terms, help them out by suggesting some of these words.

DISCUSSION: Use the analogy of the inventor who first asks "why" and then defines "what." Help individuals identify "why I do this" and just exactly "what I should do to do it better." Aim for several "I" statements form each person. Go around and around again until everyone has responded appropriately. Suggest that this is the beginning of reinventing yourself, and that they should introspectively continue this process of asking "why" first whenever they face a renewal challenge.

Some of the kinds of questions the group might consider are: Why is this procedure necessary?; Why do I do my work in the place where I do it?; Why is my work-related learning in the state it's in?; Why do I account for time/expenditures the way I do?; Why do I seek the approval of those who are my role models?; Why can't someone else do this?; etc. As the facilitator or meeting leader, you can ask these questions rhetorically, or you could write them out on a whiteboard or flipchart for all to see.

It's easy during re-engineering to focus exclusively on the big things-- the global processes, the large systems, and the organization-wide process-es that all need to be strategically aligned. Often the individual gets lost in the grandiose visions and massive change focus of many re-engineer-ing efforts. Use this exercise to bring attention down to the individual level. It's a good contrast to the "thinking big" that is the more typical approach.

The use of "I" statements is a technique borrowed from the field of psychological counseling or therapy.   It is a familiar technique to those who have been involved in sorting out relationships, as well as to those who are dealing with addictive behaviors that sabotage change efforts.

MATERIALS: Flipchart or whiteboard and markers.

TIME REQUIRED: 15 minutes - 1 hour.

17. SO, WHAT'S THE QUESTION?

from Section 1, GAMES FOR PROCESS RE-DESIGN

OBJECTIVES: To encourage humorous risk taking as prologue to a more serious idea-generating session on process re-design.

To find "the question" in a multiple-choice type exercise by examining only the answers. In testing lingo, this is a derivation of the stem from examination of the options. (Taking a multiple-choice test usually goes the other way!)

PROCEDURE: Use this as an energizer during a dull or drawn-out planning meeting, especially one in which you want participants to be more creative and vocal.

Prior to the meeting, enlist the help of a creative thinker whom you can trust not to give away the exercise before you've had a chance to do it. Sit down with this person to develop several multiple-choice test items that would be fun and a creative challenge for that particular meeting. Try to give option cues that relate to processes that could be changed for the better. Here are examples:

1.   a. accurately
      b. hurriedly
      c. at your discretion
      d. slowly
1. So, what's the question? _____

_____?

The question might be any of these:
· E-mail inquiries should be responded to?_____
· Irate customers should be answered?_____
· Requests for floating holiday time off should be submitted?_____

67

2.　　a. play it safe
　　　　b. point to someone else
　　　　c. protect what can protect you
　　　　d. keep your eyes open and your mouth shut
2. So, what's the question?_____

_____?

The question might be any of these:
- When a competitor seems to have stolen your idea, what do you do?_____
- Your department is over budget and you think you know why. The boss asks you directly what you think? What do you do?_____
- The re-engineering consultant has consistently overreported his time in the organization and asks you to sign his voucher. Do you...?_____

Do the exercise as an oral exercise by just asking the group to listen as you say the options; suggest that they write them down for reference. Or, write the options on a flipchart or whiteboard. Add energy to the exercise by creating timed competition to see who can derive the most questions within a certain time.

DISCUSSION:　　This exercise is a good way to get both the good and the bad out on the table at once. You'll be surprised at how easy it will be to identify the bad processes in need of fixing. You'll also be surprised at how clever and creative people can be when they are prodded into thinking backwards like this. Use the heightened creative level to lead onward into discussion of more serious design issues.

This kind of creativity exercise encourages flexibility and originality. Its theoretical base is in problem-solving literature.

MATERIALS:　　Possibly a flipchart or whiteboard and markers; several options lists assembled prior to the meeting.

TIME REQUIRED:　3 -5 minutes per list of options.

18. 10% VS. 90%

from Section 1, GAMES FOR PROCESS RE-DESIGN

OBJECTIVE: To focus on the differences between a Total Quality
               Management (TQM) approach and a Re-engineering
               approach to process redesign.

PROCEDURE: This is an unscrambling game to use at the beginning of a
               re-engineering thrust in an organization. It works best at a
               group meeting or in a team setting.

               Give each participant a 10% vs. 90% handout to use as a
               worksheet (see page 71). Instruct them to unscramble the
               terms, finding an appropriate place for each in either the 10%
               column or the 90% column. Suggest that experience shows
               that TQM efforts generally involve about a 10% continuous
               improvement, while Re-engineering efforts often result in a
               90% radical improvement. This worksheet is a dramatic
               illustration of the differences in approach.

               Here are the answers:
               This is the preferred placement. When all persons have
               finished unscrambling, discuss the placement of terms with
               the group, seeing how many got them all correct. Facilitate a
               discussion of the contrast between the two columns.

10% TQM	90% Re-engineering
• top management involvement at beginning	• top management involvement throughout
• improvement of current ways	• change to new ways
• incremental change	• major breakthrough
• information system as a tactical tool	• information system as a strategic tool
• slow pace	• fast pace
• from the bottom up	• from the top down
• continuous measurement	• outcome measurement
• workable with limited financial resources	• seldom works with limited financial resources

               list adapted from an article by Richard Y. Chang,
               "Improve Processes, Reengineer Them, or Both?"
               in **Training & Development**, March 1994, pp. 54ff.

DISCUSSION: In order to prevent re-engineering efforts from being characterized as "the program of the month" -- much as TQM in previous years has often been seen-- you will need to help people to understand why and how both of these massive efforts at improvement can succeed.

This kind of exercise has its roots in cognition studies, in which the study of opposites helps to define either option. Clarification of what something **is not** generally helps to clarify what exactly it is.

In your discussion, try to help people see that, in general, a useful memory device is the 10% vs 90% idea. TQM is continuous and built upon present processes; Re-engineering is abrupt and radical. One is not the other.

Imposing change of either the continuous improvement variety or the radical reengineering variety is never easy. Numerous studies about both indicate that more than half of either kind of effort fail. One of the reasons for this failure often is that the ordinary people who have to live through the changes don't really understand the goals, measurements, or characteristics of the overall change. This game helps promote that understanding.

The American Society for Training and Development (ASTD) has available a series of article reprints on organizational change from recent issues of its **Training & Development** magazine. These are available as a package for $15 through ASTD Customer Service, Box 1443, Alexandria, VA 22313 or by phoning ASTD at (703) 683-8100.

MATERIALS: An unscrambling worksheet, 10% vs 90% (page 71) for each participant; pencils.

TIME REQUIRED: 15 minutes.

UNSCRAMBLING GAME: 10% vs. 90%

top management involvement at beginning

continuous measurement

information system as a tactical tool

workable with limited financial resources

slow pace

improvement of current ways

outcome measurement

top management involvement throughout

from the top down

major breakthrough

information system as a strategic tool

fast pace

incremental change

from the bottom up

change to new ways

seldom workable with limited financial resources

Instructions: Place each term above in the appropriate column below.

10% TQM

-
-
-
-
-
-
-

90% RE-ENGINEERING

-
-
-
-
-
-
-

19. THIS IS ALL I KNOW
from Section 1, GAMES FOR PROCESS RE-DESIGN

OBJECTIVE: To provide a crutch or vehicle for helping people to be able to express their gut intuitions about how things work.

PROCEDURE: This is a homework assignment. It is meant to be done alone at a quiet time and place for reflection. It is like writing in a journal.

At the end of a team or department meeting, make the assignment: "to write down, in your own handwriting, everything you know about_____" (a specific problem). Suggest that they focus on "how things happen."   Set a time and place for collection of the papers.

DISCUSSION: These are some of the kinds of things to write about:
"All I know is ..."
"All I know is that when Joe sends me e-mail, I don't bother reading it." "All I know is that whenever I go to a team meeting, I automatically turn off."
"This is because..."
"This is because he uses e-mail to dump all over everybody and I can't be bothered with dealing with that attitude." "This is because team meetings never seem to have any agenda or focus. We all just sit around and tell each other how great we are."
"I'm not convinced that..."
"I'm not convinced that e-mail communication is good for everything. Maybe we should have some e-mail guidelines and on-line manners tips to make this kind of communication work better. Maybe I have bad on-line manners; maybe Joe does." "I'm not convinced that the team approach should be used in every situation. When it is used, we still need an agenda even if it's just a discussion agenda, and it would be better if every team meeting was totally focused on solving a specific problem."

73

Add as many other "intuition prod" fill-in-the-blank statements as you can think of in order to yield information about how people are really thinking about things.

Collect the papers at the appointed time, read them yourself or share with the group, and take action regarding process re-design based on the gut level design clues you see in front of you.

People often need opportunities to say things the way they want to say them. A narrative writing with a bit of structure can bring out process redesign issues in a way that other more "official" or formal statements can't do. When people have to be concerned with memo-type writing or being sure that they have complete sentences and good business English, they often lose touch with their intuition and write in a "protective" style. Use this exercise to help get at that intuitive understanding that most people have about how they act at work.

MATERIALS: Several " This is all I know____ " questions.

TIME REQUIRED: 10 - 30 minutes.

20. TOUGH LOVE
from Section 1, GAMES FOR PROCESS RE-DESIGN

OBJECTIVE: To use the concept of "Tough Love," that familiar approach to parenting known to anyone with a two-year-old or a fifteen-year-old, to help identify some of the difficult process changes associated with re-engineering.

PROCEDURE: This exercise is useful at the beginning of a meeting on process re-design, particularly the tough kind of re-design that often comes with re-engineering. It is a simple question and answer exercise typically led by a team leader at a flipchart.

The point you want to make is that change to the new way of doing things will feel like "tough love" -- caring harder in order to drive change. Begin by writing "TOUGH LOVE" at the top of a flipchart sheet for all to see. Continue by writing several "tough love" phrases, and encourage the group to keep thinking of more. Fill up the page with their ideas. Then go into your regular meeting agenda, having gotten participants to refocus their thinking into the "tough love" frame of reference.

DISCUSSION: Here are some ideas for "tough love" processes:
- forget the past
- make noise
- reward results; don't reward trying
- keep score
- count dollars

Keep discussion going as long as it takes to get participants to spell out the really tough kinds of attitude change they'll need as planning progresses.

There's a difference between real business imperatives and just "good words." The challenge in re-engineering is to identify the avenues to viable change.

MATERIALS: Flipchart and marker.

TIME REQUIRED: 5 minutes at the beginning of a meeting.

21. 20/20

OBJECTIVE: To engage in a rating game of descriptive characteristics of the organization in order to assess more accurately whether the organization should be in a "futuring" mode or a "planning" mode.

PROCEDURE: This is a pencil-and-paper exercise, to be used anytime during a meeting, to begin or end a meeting, or as a "back-in-your-office" exercise. Give one 20/20 RATING SCALE (photocopy page 79) to each participant. Refer to the analogy of having perfect 20/20 *vision* as they tackle this exercise. Agree on a date as the target date of the exercise.

If you "administer" the rating scale in a group setting, read aloud through several items while participants write down their ratings, to be sure they understand how to do it. Then let them finish it on their own. After everyone has completed the rating scale, begin a discussion about their ratings. Share ideas and reasons behind the ratings. Get consensus on what should be the organization's position on each item.

DISCUSSION: This is actually a "futuring" exercise in disguise. By asking the question, "Where do you think we should be?" along each continuum, you'll get people thinking about what's possible in organizational change. By including the more down-to-earth planning characteristics, that is, by creating a differential scale, you will also keep an element of reality in the exercise.

Use this exercise only as a lead-in to more serious futuring or planning. If the profile comes out more to the futuring side of center, take this as a cue to probe further and take the group into real leaps of organizational imagination.

Futuring exercises are helpful as long as participants can see some relationship to reality in doing them. True innovation must be accepted in an organization, otherwise all the creative thinking in the world won't get translated into action. Exercises like this one help on the path to innovation.

MATERIALS: A 20/20 RATING SCALE (page 79) for each participant; pencils.

TIME REQUIRED: 5 - 10 minutes.

20/20 RATING SCALE

<u>Instructions:</u> Place an X on each line indicating your assessment of where the organization *should be* on each item. Add additional items that are appropriate to your organization.

"By this date, _____, I envision that this organization should be......":

		PLANNING				**FUTURING**
		_____	____	____	____	____	____

PLANNING	FUTURING					
1. decision mode	creating mode	_____	____	____	____	____	____
2. methodical	imaginative	_____	____	____	____	____	____
3. disciplined	loose	_____	____	____	____	____	____
4. analytical	intuitive	_____	____	____	____	____	____
5. setting targets	still searching	_____	____	____	____	____	____
6. focused	fuzzy	_____	____	____	____	____	____
7. left brained	right brained	_____	____	____	____	____	____
8. segmented	flowing	_____	____	____	____	____	____
9. exclusive	inclusive	_____	____	____	____	____	____
10. private	public	_____	____	____	____	____	____

SECTION 2:
GAMES FOR INTEGRATED SYSTEMS

GAMES FOR INTEGRATED SYSTEMS
Section Overview

Staying on top of change requires a clear perspective of both the "big picture" of an organization's growth and the details of its day-to-day practices. Systems are the glue that hold organizations together, focusing on processes and "loops" of action. Systems of all sorts generally feature a "find it and fix it" approach to organizational development and a balancing of the short-term work of the present with the long-term possibilities for the future. Systems typically have phases such as analysis, design and development, action and implementation, monitoring and evaluation. Change affects every phase of a system, and seeing a system from an accurate perspective is necessary in order for the system to be able to help drive, or *support* the change.

A study of systems has always been a fascination for those interested in organizational viability. Systems, generally, by everyone's definition, are more about processes than they are about outputs. A systems approach is usually full of tools and techniques for identifying, defining, analyzing, synthesizing, and evaluating. Systems fit processes into their big pictures. Organizational change on both big and small scales demands that processes be integrated within whatever "personality" the system has.

Often this kind of integration is not the case: poor communication, lack of skills, limited vision, inefficient workflow, quality problems, attitude problems, inaduate self-assessment, and an out-of-date organizational culture all get in the way. Games in this section give you some tools for shaping integrated systems.

22. ALL THE WORLD'S A STAGE
from Section 2, GAMES FOR INTEGRATED SYSTEMS

OBJECTIVE: To use the metaphors of a dramatic play as well as the on-stage and backstage roles found in a theatrical production to help identify the current systems in place in an organization.

PROCEDURE: This is a focusing exercise best led by a facilitator at a flipchart or whiteboard. It can also be done as a verbal, question-and-answer exercise at the beginning of a planning session.

     Suggest to the group that each one recall a play in which he or she was a participant, either as an actor or in some backstage capacity. If anyone has not been in a play, suggest that they imagine what it must be like to be part of a theatrical production. Suggest that each person in the group identify with some role that is necessary to make the production a success. Remember, "All the world's a stage!"

     Go around the group asking each person in turn to tell the group which role he or she has chosen. Say the role out loud. After all persons have identified their roles, go around again, asking each person why that role is important, and what it takes for that role to contribute its best to the production. Aim for descriptions of processes that must work together.

DISCUSSION: After the group has gotten a good sense of roles and processes, ask them to switch their thinking to the processes at work and the roles people assume to make the processes all work together as a system. This time, have a free-wheeling discussion, encouraging anyone to speak up with ideas. Write the ideas on a flipchart or whiteboard. The aim of this exercise is to identify the parts of the system currently in place. Keep narrowing or expanding people's ideas until they can see clearly the parts of the system that make up their culture. Try to steer them away from simply mentioning the functional departments (accounting, public

85

relations, R&D, sales, etc.). If they need help, suggest things like finding information, building alliances, setting price, listening to customers, establishing personal credibility, etc.

Then encourage them to think in terms of the roles each one typically plays, roles such as supporter, facilitator, leader, monitor, driver, evaluator. Write these names of roles on the flipchart or whiteboard also. (Use two flipcharts for more drama-- one for the processes, and one for the roles.) Conclude the exercise by playing "What If" games-- that is, what if you in your role as a "monitor," in addition to monitoring work as usual, also had to "establish your personal credibility."

Find out how the person would go about that process; find out what other processes could be identified and what the pieces of the system are. Keep the discussion focused on identification and analysis; save the problem solving for later. Good system design begins with a realistic analysis of parts. That's what this exercise is all about!

Some analysts like to give a name to their system, after they've accurately identified the parts of the system. These system names, again, are descriptors-- helpful identifiers and modifiers that assist planners and change makers. As you continue through this exercise, you might hear comments like, "What we're really talking about is a *political* system"; or, "Sounds to me just about the same as a *family*"; or, "It's like *anthropology* around here"; or, "Yes, it is like a Wagnerian *drama*." Continue to use metaphor and analogy as crutches to identification. You'll be surprised at how creative your team can be! Encourage the expansion of the metaphors as long as they are productive in getting your group to realistic definition of system parts. This is the first step toward integration.

MATERIALS: Flipchart or whiteboard and markers.

TIME REQUIRED: 10 - 20 minutes.

23. DON'T SHOOT THE MESSENGER

from Section 2, GAMES FOR INTEGRATED SYSTEMS

OBJECTIVE: To use the familiar slogan, "Don't shoot the messenger!" as a framework for beginning the system's evaluation design.

PROCEDURE: This is an exercise in which subordinates (or team members) report back to a supervisor or team leader on an ongoing basis. A poster, similar to the one found on page 89, should be available in a prominent and accessible place in the leader's office. As bad news is discovered, anyone discovering it writes out the bad news on the poster. At a specified time, such as 2 weeks from now, the poster full of bad news becomes the reference document from which to design a system evaluation plan. It should be taken to a group or team meeting for all to see. Add additional pages as needed.

DISCUSSION: Use this slogan as a way into discussion of process evaluation that leads to design of system evaluation. Keep in mind that results of evaluation, in a systems framework, always are used to make the system better. Evaluation flows from the implementation phases of a system; and it's in the details of implementation where the bad news originates.

Messengers of bad news need to know that they are performing a valuable service in uncovering the raw material for honest evaluation that leads into improvement. It's the bringing of bad news that helps to determine evaluation standards; all messengers need to know that their processes of bringing the news are valuable.

One of the biggest obstacles to the good uses of evaluation information is the tendency of leaders to aim at the nearest target and shoot the messenger who brings bad news. Let this poster remind you to change your "shoot the messenger" behavior!

MATERIALS: A "DON'T SHOOT THE MESSENGER" poster (page 89).

TIME REQUIRED: About one minute of time to make a note on the poster.

Inca King's Runner, Bolivia

DON'T SHOOT THE MESSENGER!

message 1
message 2
message 3
message 4
message 5

24. HORSE TRADING
from Section 2, GAMES FOR INTEGRATED SYSTEMS

OBJECTIVE: To give persons a skill for gaining acceptance of a new approach or idea when seeking system integration.

PROCEDURE: "Horse trading" is a verbal trick to be pulled out of your facilitator's hat at any appropriate moment as people are moving through change. It has another common name, "You scratch my back and I'll scratch yours." It sometimes is referred to in its more sophisticated form as "trading up." It often finds a companion in "What's in it for me?" It means that as you gather support for a change, you ask for help (budget help, influence, favors) from key persons along the way, in return for promise of support from the change for their own pet projects. Horse trading is a way of dealing.

DISCUSSION: As a facilitator or team leader, don't hesitate to remind people of this ancient-- and mostly honorable-- personal negotiating technique.

The "trading up" variation is for the more experienced "dealer." In trading up, you consciously build a support system by gathering a piece of key information and then sharing it selectively with the person next in line, always trading upward for information and influence. Obviously in all of this, the persons involved must be operating under valid, positive, organizational goals for growth.

Two excellent reference books deal with personal skills required to drive change. The classic is Rosabeth Moss Kanter's **The Change Masters**, New York: Touchstone, Simon & Schuster, 1984, especially chapter 8, "Power Skills in Use: Corporate Entrepreneurs in Action," pp.209 ff. The other is Peter Scott-Morgan's **The Unwritten Rules of the Game**, New York: McGraw-Hill, Inc., 1994.

MATERIALS: None.

TIME REQUIRED: About one minute.

25. INITIATION RITE

from Section 2, GAMES FOR INTEGRATED SYSTEMS

OBJECTIVE: To help build commitment to making change work.

PROCEDURE: Near the end of the system phase generally known as design or development, and right before implementation begins, create some "initiation rite" for those willing souls who will pioneer forward with you through the change. In the following schematic, the initiation rite should come where the arrow indicates:

analysis...design/development...implementation...evaluation

Devise any kind of ritual that works in your organizational context. Make it meaningful, symbolic, one-shot, and showy. Some suggestions are: take the committed people up in a hot air balloon; go together on an "Outward Bound"-type program; participate in a Native American Sweat Lodge or Vision Quest; or do something at the worksite like plant a tree, or purchase Ficus, Yucca, or other hardy office trees for each person who's bought in to the change.

DISCUSSION: The concept of "membership" is an important psychological notion that takes a person forward to integration and a feeling of accomplishment. The importance of "belonging" in a group was popularized by psychologist Abraham H. Maslow of Brandeis University way back in the 1950's. His theories of motivation and personality have informed educational psychology for decades. The act of an initiation rite at the formal beginning of change implementation helps to confirm membership and build commitment to making the change work.

Another very useful little book is **Firing Up Commitment During Organizational Change** by Price Pritchett, 1994. Books can be ordered by phoning Pritchett & Associates in Dallas, TX at 800-992-5922.

MATERIALS: Initiation rite materials for each person making a commitment
                  to implementing the change (tickets, reservations, plants,
                  etc.).

TIME REQUIRED: Varied; from several minutes to several days.

26. MANAGE THE TRANSITION

from Section 2, GAMES FOR INTEGRATED SYSTEMS

OBJECTIVE: To use a model of change management as a crutch in dealing with the problem of keeping control of systems in transition.

PROCEDURE: This is a template exercise, that is, a kind of approach that generally appeals to the planners and left-brained people in your organization. In it, you provide change drivers with a model for change, and encourage them to fit themselves into the model. The model below is one kind of template; use this or develop your own template based on unique character-istics of your organization.

step 1	step 2	step 3	step 4
Describe a clear image of the future.	Use leverage points.	Redefine the functions in the organization.	Structure the frequent use of feedback.

(adapted from Richard Beckhard & Reuben Harris, Organizational Transitions, Reading, MA: Addison-Wesley, 1987)

Draw your template on a flipchart or whiteboard if you are in a group setting. Otherwise, simply use it yourself or as a dialogue device in a one to one situation.

DISCUSSION: The four major areas of transition management can be seen as vision, leverage, re-work, and feedback. Encourage your planners and change managers to identify the transition state and to use a template device or organizational development model as they take control of systems in transition.

The field of organizational development (OD) is full of models, many of which were developed and expanded in the 1970s, when the field blossomed. Among the academics and practitioners writing at that time were Warren Bennis, John Kotter, David Nadler, Tom Peters, and Victor Vroom. Libraries and on-line data bases are full of their work which has defined the field from that day to the present. Many people like to work with models; you can't go wrong by using any of these sources.

MATERIALS: A model of transition management and a flipchart,
                  whiteboard, or paper on which to draw it; markers.

TIME REQUIRED: 2 - 15 minutes.

27. MARCHING ORDERS
from Section 2, GAMES FOR INTEGRATED SYSTEMS

OBJECTIVE: To label and organize paper footprints with processes that build integrated systems.

PROCEDURE: Use this game in a workshop where you want participants to be mildly physically active. It can be effectively used at slow times such as after lunch, or at 3 o'clock in the afternoon when energy is low.

Photocopy the footprint patterns on page 99 onto brightly colored copy paper and cut them out. Make enough so that each participant has about a dozen of each size footprint. Have a pile of extras available too. At the beginning of the exercise, give each person a stack of footprints of various colors.

The task is to identify a major business process or service and break it down into "steps," that is, the individual parts of the system which have to lead logically into each other in order for that process or service to be accomplished. Each footprint gets one step only.

For experienced planners, you might want to further delimit the exercise by suggesting that all analysis steps must be in hot pink, all design steps in sunshine yellow, all implementation steps in lime green, all evaluation and feedback steps in royal blue.

In groups where time or expertise is limited, you could focus only on one critical part of the system, such as evaluation and feedback. In this situation, use only the processes of evaluation and feedback, defining them in detail.

Another variation of the exercise for a large group is to break into subgroups, each small group working on only one phase of the system.

Keep in mind that the objective is to organize the footprints in logical order after the labeling is done. When you get to this point, clear away a large floor space so that the system can be laid out on the floor. Have everyone get up at once, arranging the footprints in the proper sequence for effective progress. If there are several identical or similar footprints, display them side by side, as in a military parade. If small differences matter, ask the creators of the prints to negotiate whose footprint should be first. Display all footprints.

DISCUSSION: Let the action carry your discussion of what it takes to make the (new) system work. Be prepared for some surprises. Try to get the footprints to eventually meet in a circle or ellipse, making the point that systems are somewhat circular. Be ready to see creative types make several circles. Keep it going as long as good ideas are forthcoming.

The work of Peter Senge in systems thinking is essential reading in the field. His best-seller, **The Fifth Discipline: The Art and Practice of the Learning Organization**, New York, Doubleday Currency, 1990, is a classic in the new thinking about organizations and systems. His newer work, in collaboration with other authors, **The Fifth Discipline Fieldbook**, Doubleday Currency, 1994, contains a chapter full of good ideas and applications about "systems thinking." See Chapter 13, "Strategies for Systems Thinking," pp.87ff.

MATERIALS: Footprints cut out from patterns on page 99.

TIME REQUIRED: 20 - 60 minutes.

MARCHING ORDERS

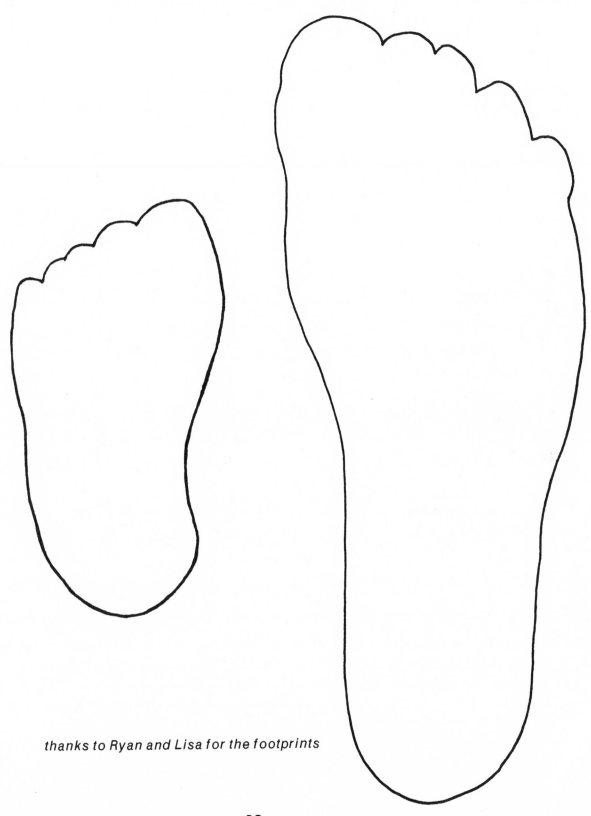

thanks to Ryan and Lisa for the footprints

99

28. PINOCCHIO
from Section 2, GAMES FOR INTEGRATED SYSTEMS

OBJECTIVE: To use a poster, replicated and strategically placed around
                   an organization, to appeal to the creative, synthesizing,
                   right-brained people on the change team.

PROCEDURE: Make copies of the Pinocchio/Jiminy Cricket poster, page
                   103, and distribute them freely around the organization's
                   offices and corridors. Let the message of the poster settle in
                   people's minds for several weeks prior to a major planning
                   session.

DISCUSSION: Discussion of the poster begins after it has been given a
                   chance to influence its viewers. When that time comes,
                   assemble your change team and dialogue about
                   organizational values. Too often in the throes of action,
                   change drivers don't take time to let things simmer. This
                   poster exercise is one that encourages the reflection,
                   synthesizing, holistic sort of approach to where the new
                   systems are headed. Give people a chance to answer the
                   implied question on the poster, that is, "What is our
                   organizational conscience?" Integrated systems don't
                   happen unless there is a clearly defined organizational
                   conscience. Use this poster as a reminder to articulate one,
                   carefully, throughout the organization.

This exercise is grounded in cognitive psychology, making use of the idea
that long-term memory can be a powerful tool as it stores lessons learned
from childhood as chunks of meaning. The reminder of the well-known
Pinocchio story can help change makers remember how important it is to
have a conscience.

MATERIALS: Pinocchio posters.

TIME REQUIRED: Several seconds to glance at a poster;
                   additional 5 - 15 minutes for discussion later.

****

ORGANIZATIONAL CONSCIENCE

****

29. ROOTS AND WINGS
from Section 2, GAMES FOR INTEGRATED SYSTEMS

OBJECTIVE: To adapt the familiar parenting motto, "The best thing you can give your child is roots and wings," for helping to build an integrated system philosophy before change strikes.

PROCEDURE: The concept of roots and wings is inherent in that first day of school, Bar Mitzvah, the Senior Prom, the semester abroad, the wedding day. Parents seeing their child through these big change events feel at a gut level that somehow they've given their child the roots of value and patterns of behavior to stay grounded during change and that they have also provided the child with hopes, visions, and skills to spread his or her wings in growth. The roots and wings metaphor is especially meaningful to a work group that contains parents. For groups that don't contain parents, the metaphor is still useful as individuals remember how their parents gave them roots and wings.

As with other powerful experience-based metaphors, this one is useful to express meaning in a holistic way, that is, all at once, without a lot of words. Use the term, "roots and wings" freely in your discussions to help people define and then develop the attitudes and skills they'll need to anticipate change and act accordingly in the meantime. Help people to see that, like child rearing, the development of organizations requires conscious strategies for teaching values and skills to weather change. Take the metaphor as far as you want to, with printed slogans, pencils, letterhead, coffee mugs, or whatever it takes to sensitize people to the need to develop value-based, long-term attitudes and skills to see the organization through to its best future.

DISCUSSION: <u>Training</u> magazine, May 1994 (p. 136) ran a column titled, "The Change Monster," in which an editor presented an analysis of a recent Gallup Organization survey of 400 executives from *Fortune* 1,000 companies on the topic of readiness for dealing with change. Results of the survey indicated, among other things, that only about half of those executives said their organizations anticipated change and acted in advance to manage it. In addition, a full 60 percent of those surveyed responded that managing the "quality and advancement of workers" was very important to the organization. Studies like these point out the need for organizations to develop both roots and wings, in anticipation of growth and change.

The notion of integrity is not reserved only for individuals. In our corporate search for quality and service, we also seek to become an entity of integrity. Integrated systems is part of this search. Metaphors such as roots and wings, from human development, can be useful in organization development.

MATERIALS: None.

TIME REQUIRED: Less than a minute at critical influence points.

30. THE SIZZLE AND THE STEAK
from Section 2, GAMES FOR INTEGRATED SYSTEMS

OBJECTIVE: To use the advertising concept of enticing consumers with both the "sizzle and the steak" when buying a product or service in order to engage change drivers in dialogue about defining the value-added components of integrated systems.

PROCEDURE: Continuously, obsessively, relentlessly keep before your change drivers the idea that added value (the "sizzle") must be designed into and delivered with every nuts-and-bolts piece (the "steak") of new systems. Apply the "sizzle and steak" concept especially to design issues.

DISCUSSION: One way to do this is to tell stories; use examples. Popular business magazines (**Business Week**, **Forbes**, **Fortune**, **Harvard Business Review**, **Training**, etc.) are full of vignettes and reports of companies and organizations of all sorts who have successfully weathered the storms of downsizing, re-engineering, and takeover to emerge stronger in some way. Chances are, if you read carefully, you'll discover that the new integrated systems, whatever they are, are characterized by some element of "value-added." **Information Week**, CPM Publications, Manhasset, NY, is an excellent source.

Two good sources of examples are the successful training manager and the successful information manager, or at highest levels, the VP HRD, and the CIO. If these folks have made it through major organizational change, chances are that they've delivered both the sizzle and the steak. Middle management, and even top management, in these two areas are particularly susceptible to being replaced by consultants, vendor services, and outsourcing. Find good examples from these areas, and you'll have no trouble convincing your change makers that integrated systems in the new organizational world demand both the sizzle and the steak.

Michael Earl and David Feeney's article, "Does the CIO Add Value?," in **Information Week**, May 30, 1994, contains a chart on page 66 suggesting six ways in which a CIO can add value. These are:

1. Focusing always on business imperatives (that is, not on just the details of the field of information services (IS))
2. Interpreting success stories from other fields in the context of IS
3. Seeking, establishing, and cultivating executive relationships (that is, don't behave like a stereotype techie)
4. Setting high and visible performance standards and promoting their achievement (don't hide behind the jargon or the "inherent superiority" of the field)
5. Focusing and concentrating the IS development effort
6. Creating a challenging vision of the role of information technology and sharing that vision throughout the company.

These six actions can apply equally to any other specialized field within a company. Substitute any other field: training, accounting, marketing, etc. Add value by behaving and thinking like business persons. It doesn't hurt to constantly remind the specialists who have survived major change that both the "sizzle and the steak" are needed as new ways of doing things are inaugurated.

MATERIALS: Several stories or examples of value-added action.

TIME REQUIRED: Several minutes to tell a story or use an example.

31. THERMOSTAT

from Section 2, GAMES FOR INTEGRATED SYSTEMS

OBJECTIVE:

To use the gimmick of the principle of a thermostat as a self-regulating device for an individual's passion (heat) for maintaining an environment that sustains change.

PROCEDURE:

This is an individual, self-monitoring game to encourage persons involved in change to keep the heat on themselves to get through the change.

Make copies of the THERMOSTAT chart on page 111 for each participant. This chart is designed for one week's worth of monitoring. Make additional charts for additional weeks. Don't burden people with this; one to three weeks is about all people can take of a game like this.

Ask them to monitor themselves in terms of their own level of "heat" for the change. Establish a setpoint of, for example, 82 degrees F, that is, just a little too warm for real comfort. Get the point across that you expect individuals to keep the heat on themselves as new systems are designed and as they begin working together in new ways. Use weather, climate, and temperature metaphors in your conversations during the time of monitoring .

At an agreed-upon time of each day, for example, at 4 p.m., have each participant stop and monitor his/her temperature for change. The object is to keep the heat on during the critical transition period. A person's profile should be scattered around the 72 - 92 degree points, indicating that the "thermostat" for change is maintaining the proper environment for well-being during this period. Occasional spikes into the freezing or feverish ranges can be expected. Making change is tough work.

DISCUSSION:

Encourage people to be honest. Also encourage them to record their comments about each particular reading. Share profiles at a group meeting to get people's frustrations and

109

feelings out in the open as you try to establish just exactly the right environment for successful change.

Living through major change is fundamentally an individual matter, so whatever you can do to encourage individuals to take charge of change will pay off for the organization in a big way. Leadership through change must be a matter of individual leadership. This game can help.

MATERIALS: A THERMOSTAT profile (page 111) for each participant.

TIME REQUIRED: A few minutes daily during the time of monitoring.

THERMOSTAT

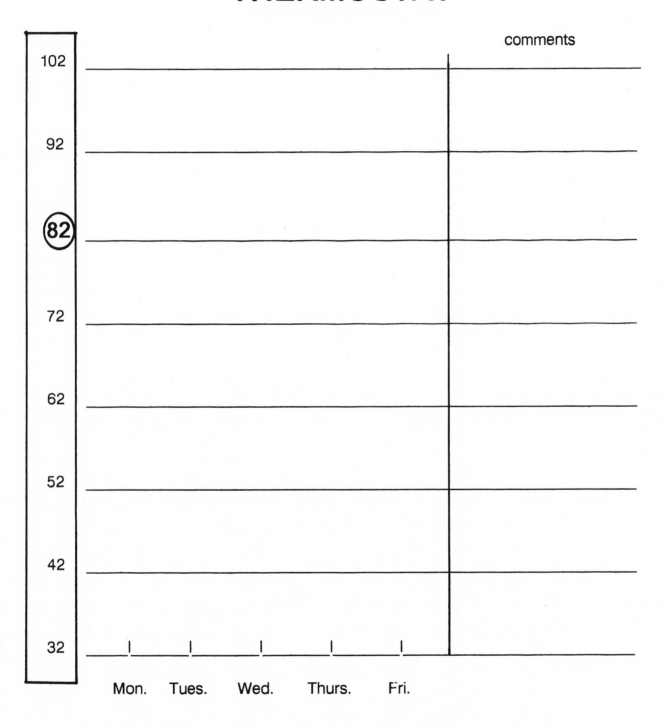

comments

102

92

82

72

62

52

42

32

Mon.   Tues.   Wed.   Thurs.   Fri.

week of:_____

32. WE THE PEOPLE
from Section 2, GAMES FOR INTEGRATED SYSTEMS

OBJECTIVE: To use the Preamble to the United States Constitution as inspiration for entering, developing, and implementing phases of system integration.

PROCEDURE: Distribute copies of the Preamble (page 115) to those on your team who are charged with developing a mission statement for the new organization as you begin trying to make the system work. Use it freely as a means to enlist commitment to changes and as a model to which everyone can relate.

DISCUSSION: The Preamble to the United States Constitution (1787) remains one of the most positive statements of organizational vision in effect today. Together with the Bill of Rights, the first ten amendments to the Constitution, it is probably the most memorized and quoted political document in our history. It doesn't hurt to review it for its wisdom and strength as a survivor and supporter of change.

The Preamble is a positive statement, unlike the Bill of Rights, which is a collection of negative statements ("Congress shall not, government shall not," etc.) When individuals have to work together in a team to put down on paper their vision for their new world, it is helpful to have models which are expressed in positive terms. It is helpful, too, to be able to contrast this positive expression with a visionary negative expression. These two major documents from our historical past can be an excellent source of inspiration and learning.

> It is useful to view systems from various perspectives, as individuals try to develop and implement new ways of acting with integrity. This "We the people..." document is a model of simplicity and elegance. It resonates with people's experience and value system as Americans.

MATERIALS: Copies of the Preamble to the US Constitution (page 115).

TIME REQUIRED: Several minutes.

WE THE PEOPLE...

Preamble to the Constitution of the United States of America
Adopted September 17, 1787; Effective March 4, 1789.

"We the people of the United States,

in order to form a more perfect union,

establish justice, insure domestic tranquillity,

provide for the common defense,

promote the general welfare, and secure the

blessings of liberty to ourselves and our posterity,

do ordain and establish this Constitution

for the United States of America."

33. WRONG FOREST
from Section 2, GAMES FOR INTEGRATED SYSTEMS

OBJECTIVES: To use the familiar metaphor of seeing the "forest and the trees" to help drive home the need to identify and define carefully. To elaborate on this metaphor by suggesting that sometimes the major problem is that one is in the "wrong forest."

PROCEDURE: Use the verbal analogy of forests and trees to help people to see the difference between minor tweaks and major fixes. Use the "wrong forest!" comment much as you would the punch line of a joke, that is, save it for the most opportune moment of "aha" experience. Use it anytime you are trying to get people to look at an issue from a different point of view.

DISCUSSION: The re-engineering literature is full of war stories about fixes that didn't work, took up enormous resources, wasted time and money, and took great tolls in terms of trust and human relationships. Often, re-engineering efforts are directed at broken or underdeveloped systems; the search for integrated systems very often runs headlong into re-engineering.

Some of the problems frequently reported are that executive leadership is not fully committed to radical change (they're in the "wrong forest"); that there is little consensus on the part of the executive group both about what business they are really in and about what magnitude of change they really want. Executives caught in this confusion need to be reminded that not only do they need to be sure about whether they're seeing the "forest" or the "trees," but they also need to know whether or not they're in the right forest.

The forest and trees metaphor comes from the field of psychology, and is a common way of introducing the concept of conceptually-driven information versus data-driven information. Like the right-brain versus left-brain simplification of explanations for the ways in which we think, the forest/trees simplification is an attempt to help people see that there are radically different ways in which to deal with issues. "Wrong forest" elaborates on this.

MATERIALS: None.

TIME REQUIRED: Less than a minute at strategic times.

34. "YO, I'M YOUR CEO!"
from Section 2, GAMES FOR INTEGRATED SYSTEMS

OBJECTIVE: To use the famous Ben & Jerry's poster contest to find a new
               CEO as a reminder that companies can grow and compete
               favorably while acting responsibly regarding the environment
               and social issues, as has Ben & Jerry's Homemade Ice
               Cream of Waterbury, Vermont .

PROCEDURE: At the start of a planning session considering re-engineered
               systems, corporate visioning, or major process change, refer
               to Ben & Jerry's well-known corporate philosophy of using
               the power of business to improve the lives of people in the
               community. If you can get a copy of Ben & Jerry's WE
               WANT YOU TO BE OUR CEO poster from June 1994, use it
               as a prop during discussion of socially responsible integrated
               systems. If not, simply describe the poster and refer to the
               widely publicized contest for a new CEO. (Associated Press,
               for example, ran a story in mid-June in numerous
               newspapers about Ben and Jerry's campaign to attract a
               "different kind" of CEO, one who would carry on their
               tradition of social responsibility.) Popular business
               magazines around that time had articles and photos of the
               contest.

               Use the Ben & Jerry experience (7.5 percent of pre-tax
               earnings to projects to benefit families and the environment,
               growth to a $140 million business in 16 years, and a current
               40 percent market share of the superpremium ice cream
               market) to illustrate that social awareness and commitment
               can be a successful part of integrated systems. Let Ben &
               Jerry's be an inspiration to your own change drivers. See for
               example, **The Berkshire Eagle,** June 14, 1994, p. D 1, and
               June 16, 1994, Editorial, A8.

DISCUSSION: Many people are very committed to preserving the
               environment and facilitating the responsible use of business
               profits to improve communities. As your people try to
               integrate socially responsible actions into their new systems,

119

help them to remember the successes of Ben & Jerry's Homemade, Inc.

Of course, there are many other companies that act in a socially responsible way. Indeed, like Ben & Jerry's Homemade, Inc., many businesses are developing mission statements that deal with the relationships between economics, society, and their products.

An interesting conference brochure crossed my own desk in mid-June 1994, advertising a National OD (Organization Development) Network conference, "Acting With Passion and Courage for Socially Responsible Change," to be held in Baltimore in October. Those who must design integrated systems should pay attention to Ben & Jerry's concept of "linked prosperity" and to conferences like this one.

MATERIALS: None; or reprints of Ben & Jerry's contest poster for CEO.

TIME REQUIRED: Several minutes of description.

SECTION 3:
GAMES FOR COMMUNICATION

GAMES FOR COMMUNICATION
Section Overview

Information movement and management throughout an organization are critical processes that drive change. The availability and volume of information through computer and telephone technologies stagger the imagination and challenge even the most astute and clever managers. What people know and when they share it are profoundly simple questions confronting all employees in all organizational structures. Communication in today's interconnected world of information is a supreme challenge in mastering change at all levels.

The following **GAMES FOR COMMUNICATION** raise issues of accessing, networking, sharing, interpreting, designing, initiating, and using information for the purpose of communication. They can help you to develop a vision for information within your organization that fosters a communication explosion as you drive change. They can help you develop high-leverage communication tools and systems.

35. COMMUNITY VS. CONTEST
from Section 3, GAMES FOR COMMUNICATION

OBJECTIVE: To dramatize the differences between building community and having a contest, and in the process of the game, to help players understand one idea in cross gender communication.

PROCEDURE: This active game requires people to move from one side of the room to another, lining up behind either the sign for "community" or the sign for "contest."

In order to do this, push tables and chairs aside so that a space large enough for moving about is created. Make and post a sign that says "COMMUNITY" and a sign that says "CONTEST" as if each were the head of a team. As you read each term (page 127), instruct people in the group to line up according to each person's affinity for the term you've just read. You'll find that very few people are clearly related to only community or only contest. Use this as a warm-up exercise prior to a serious discussion of communication issues surrounding gender differences.

DISCUSSION: Clearly, a major communication issue of our times is the issue of cross gender communication in the workplace. Volumes have been written and thousands of seminars have been attended to foster understanding among the sexes at work. New terms such as "a victim mentality," "culture of blame," "empowerment versus dependency," and "driving out fear" have become part of our business language parlance. We say that we seek candor, honesty, and responsibility for self in our dealings with each other.

The important message to convey in this game is that change for the better in cross gender communication will not be accomplished by changing the other person; rather, it will happen because each person will learn to better *explain* his or her point of view and be willing to *interpret* another's messages. The aim, of course, is to appreciate and understand men and women at work, within the complex of changing power and authority issues in the workplace.

125

Deborah Tannen, Ph.D., best-selling author of gender difference books, coined the term "genderlect," a term akin to the word "dialect," meaning an established and largely unchangeable way of talking. Her book, **You Just Don't Understand: Women and Men in Conversation**, NY: Random House, 1990, is especially useful. In it, she suggests that women generally are about building community and men generally are about having a contest. These two essential gender differences affect communication.

Recent court cases have also been instructive: Anita Hill vs. Clarence Thomas, and Rena Weeks vs. Baker & McKenzie. Litigation on both sides of both cases was full of misunderstanding and failed communication. As the **New York Times** (7/29/94, p. B7) says, "'This is a wake-up call about what can happen if you don't have your act together.'"

St. Francis of Assisi asked to be made "an instrument of peace"; Henry Higgins exclaimed in exasperation, "Why can't a woman be more like a man?!" (My Fair Lady). Communication between people has been historically confounded by gender differences. The issue is not to erase these differences, but to understand them. This game can be an instrument to help achieve that understanding.

MATERIALS: List of contrasting terms; signs "COMMUNITY" and "CONTEST" to post at the head of two "teams".

TIME REQUIRED: 5 - 10 minutes.

126

community   *contest*

Ask the question: Do you relate more to this... or that...? Read the terms and point to the corresponding sign as you do. Get people moving after each pair of terms.

1. Why haven't you dealt with this?   or   Why should I deal with this?

2. Customers should be listened to.   or   Customers adore her.

3. Find out why his numbers are off.   or   He's had a tough quarter.

4. I need to talk to you about his behavior.   or   No way is that harassment.

5. Live by the model.   or   Camouflage the model.

6. Face the problem.   or   Keep smiling.

7. Accept the consequences.   or   Always be a cheerleader.

Add more pairs, as appropriate.

36. CRUSADE

from Section 3, GAMES FOR COMMUNICATION

OBJECTIVE: To redirect an individual's shaken self-worth after initial stages of change.

PROCEDURE: This is a flipchart exercise led by a facilitator. The point in facilitation is to help people refocus on the higher level "causes" -- that is, embark on a crusade-- and thereby help them to see that personal achievement and success are possible again, even in a new unconquered land.

Use two flipcharts, side by side, one labeled "WOUNDS" and the other, "CRUSADE." Copy the list of "wounds" (add any others of your own) onto the lefthand flipchart. Reserve the righthand flipchart for the challenges of the "crusade." Read the list of words, one by one, recording corresponding challenges on the crusade flipchart. Go for at least a one to one correspondence; force people to bring each "wound" to a higher level.

WOUNDS	CRUSADE
1. criticism about my work habits 2. being left out of decisions 3. restricted access to leaders 4. lack of financial data 5. exclusion from results meetings 6. no merit pay 7. privileged parking eliminated 8. reduction in expense account etc.	

Example: For "wound" number 1, a corresponding "crusade" item might be: Let's operate under rules of giving and receiving feedback.

129

DISCUSSION: Continue discussing and identifying higher level challenges.
                 List as many as you can for each "wound." Early in the
                 implementation of change, help individuals recognize the
                 personal challenges ahead. Help them to restore their faith in
                 themselves and in the organization's mission.

                 People need to feel needed and useful; people need to
                 achieve. Communicate this early in the change process, and
                 your "crusaders" can help drive the change.

> Much has been written lately about the demise of loyalty.
> Capitalize on the tendency of human nature to want to work for
> causes, in spite of this apparent trend.   Because of the nature
> of the times, don't expect people to want to work for a company,
> a particular boss, or a brand name.
>
> Use the analogy of a diving or golf scorecard, wherein a per-
> son competes against his or her own best score. Individual
> self-worth sometimes needs to be rejuvenated during change,
> and often, communication exercises like this one, directed at
> individuals, can help. Individual self-worth will be the founda-
> tion for a renewed commitment to corporate mission.

MATERIALS: Two flipcharts, markers, and a list of "WOUNDS".

TIME REQUIRED: 5 - 15 minutes.

37. EXPO

from Section 3, GAMES FOR COMMUNICATION

OBJECTIVES: To share ideas, methods, and products among internal groups or departments. To exchange "how to" information internally in an effort to communicate work processes and work products.

PROCEDURE: Turn your cafeteria, lunchroom, or library into an "Expo" demonstration area similar to the Expos at trade shows and conventions. This one, however, is for internal exposure only-- no customers or outsiders permitted.

Follow the standard Expo format of booths or tabletop exposition areas where creators and "sellers" of products and services can gather to promote their wares. Staff each booth or table with friendly, knowledgeable developers who can answer questions about their work. Have work samples on hand for demonstration and perusal.

Schedule an Expo Day (or afternoon) when employees are free to wander around and ask questions. Use the time for people to follow their interests, not necessarily their own current line of work.

DISCUSSION: Following the Expo, meet in regular work groups to talk about the good ideas people gathered. Keep discussion upbeat and focused on what was outstanding or what people learned.

> Adapt standard Expo presentation tricks-- videos, giveaways, contests, hands-on action, food-- make it a festive event. Invite families. A little joy never hurt communication!

MATERIALS: Samples of work products and services; Expo materials and room setup.

TIME REQUIRED: 2 - 3 hours.

131

38. HERD RIDER
from Section 3, GAMES FOR COMMUNICATION

OBJECTIVE: To deliberately set up a "communication node" in the form of a person who freely roams around the organization to spot communication problems and to devise creative solutions to them.

PROCEDURE: Rotate herd rider assignments among all members of your organization, for example, each person assumes the herd rider role for a two-week period. Suggest that a percentage of that person's time, such as two hours per day (25%) for that period, be devoted to herd rider activities. Suggest that the herd rider contribute to an organizational journal, a three-ring binder that contains the cumulative ideas and observations of all herd riders. The focus of all herd riders is the same:identification of communication problems and design of solutions to them. Keep the herd riding activity in the realm of creativity; don't be too quick to plan and actually solve the problems. Focus on the up-front aspects of creative analysis.

DISCUSSION: This game works well in an organization that has had some experience with empowered teams and lowered levels of authority. Officially giving the analysis and documentation power to one person at a time helps to develop each person's analysis skill-- like brainstorming in three-dimension!

Some of the communication problems in flatter organizations, where information is supremely accessible, have to do with the appropriate people getting the appropriate information. Knowledge is king in contemporary organizations; sometimes an interested third party (i.e., the herd rider) can very effectively identify the when, how, and why of building that knowledge base.

MATERIALS: The herd rider's schedule.

TIME REQUIRED: A prescribed time out of each week's work schedule for riding herd, for example, 25% of time for three months in order to accomplish the goal of communication problem analysis.

133

39. IT'S WARM IN HERE
from Section 3, GAMES FOR COMMUNICATION

OBJECTIVES: To sensitize people to various styles of communication during typical business conversation; to identify those styles present in one's own company and to place them in some kind of communication matrix or model. To use the title of this exercise as a reminder to say what you mean: that is, *not* to say "It's warm in here" when what you really mean to say is "Would you mind if I opened the window a crack to let in some fresh air?" Use the title to suggest the dysfunctional communication games we often play with each other without thinking.

PROCEDURE: This is a flipchart exercise, or one to be done at a blackboard or whiteboard so that all participants can see what is being written.   It can form the basis of a workshop in communication for workgroups or teams.

Begin in brainstorming fashion, that is, each comment is valid and none is criticized as it is given. Ask the group to think about and then try to identify the different communication styles present in the company. Write each different style down so that all can see. (The wording may be modified as the exercise continues, if all agree.) After each person has contributed something and new ideas seem to be exhausted, try to categorize or organize the styles into some matrix or model. Follow with ideas for making communication better.

DISCUSSION: There are many communication models to follow. One of the latest is that described in Peter Senge et al.'s new **Fifth Discipline Fieldbook**, NY: Doubleday Currency, 1994, pages 253-259. This particular model suggests a balance between "advocacy" and "inquiry," that is, a balance between the directive and assertive kinds of conversational communication associated with old style managers and the newer conversational styles that probe and listen and reflect.

Senge describes 13 communication styles including, "testing, explaining, interrogating, clarifying, politicking," and so forth.

135

He organizes the various styles into a 2 x 2 matrix . Follow a similar pattern or organization, or make up your own. Another good reference is John W. Newstrom's and Jon L. Pierce's **Windows Into Organizations**, NY: Amacom, 1990. The goal is to get people to see that various conversational styles are always at work, and that some are more appropriate and more functional than others. Use either of these references as background reading for discussion.

Individuals develop communication styles all during their lives. A person's style is affected by criticism and praise, the need to please or to achieve, and a host of other psychological influences during childhood and adult development. New ways of working require changes in communication style. The first step toward change is analysis, definition, and understanding. This exercise helps.

MATERIALS: Flipchart and markers.

TIME REQUIRED: 20 minutes - 1 hour.

40. JURASSIC BUGS

from Section 3, GAMES FOR COMMUNICATION

OBJECTIVE: To use absurdity to illuminate the work measurement problems so often inherent in computer-generated work.

PROCEDURE: The goal of this game is to articulate each absurdity in measurement or communication currently being experienced by workers. Do this by running a "contest" over the course of a week or two in which individuals are given the task of making up a "rule" that is related to a current work rule but is expressed as an absurdity.

For example, for the software development department in which errors per line of code is the evaluation standard for individual workers, revise the standard to say, "Spur-of-the-moment meetings per lines of code." This, obviously, is an absurd measurement standard, but it has an element of truth in it about work behavior: that is, when a developer is creating lines of code, progress and efficiency definitely suffer when team leaders or managers call impromptu meetings. The communication message in creating this "Jurassic Bug" is to figure out what is of value (perhaps the meetings *are* of value) and discard any outdated ("Stone Age") measurement standards.

At some predetermined time, call an end to the contest and gather all rewritten rules for a general free-for-all discussion. Give out prizes (dinosaur pencils or erasers from a toy store) to outstanding absurdities.

DISCUSSION: Changing times demand changing monitoring and measuring systems and standards. Numbers have always been important in measurement and evaluation, but they often cloud communication. Even the industrial efficiency experts so popular forty years ago knew that numerical quotas often distort the way people work (**Information Week**, July 18, 1994, p.48). Statistics are easy to manipulate to "prove" almost anything.

137

During discussion, and prior to the start of the contest if necessary, remind people that electronic monitoring affects all kinds of employees: clerks, typists, airline reservation agents and others who schedule, switchboard operators, factory workers, stockbrokers, those who deal with volumes of data as well as those who deal with volumes of people. **Information Week** (op. cit.) notes that by the mid-1980s, nearly two-thirds of U.S. workers who worked at computer terminals were electronically monitored for numbers of pages, numbers of keystrokes, and amounts of time. Docket sheets followed everybody everywhere, and those with privileged access could find out all of the numbers at any time.

Encourage your "contestants" to think creatively about work standards and measurements, and in the process, contribute significantly to driving change about evaluation.

This game is part analysis and part creative problem solving. The analysis piece of it is hard for many people because you are asking them to do a self-analysis within an organizational analysis, and it's hard for people to be objective and remove themselves to a "third-party" position. The creative problem solving is sometimes hard for people too, but with a bit of encouragement (hence, the contest format), they can experiment with creative thinking such as using analogies, juxtaposition, riddles, absurdity, and play on words.

The game is especially useful because it is focused on both evaluation and communication.

MATERIALS: None.

TIME REQUIRED: A minute or two per day of thinking time during the contest; about half an hour for reporting back and discussion later.

41. MEDIA CREATION
from Section 3, GAMES FOR COMMUNICATION

OBJECTIVES: To realize the danger in accepting stereotypes; to analyze and define the internal "media creations" within an organization; to use the stereotypes about "Generation X" as an example of what media creation can do and why thinking people should be wary.

PROCEDURE: This exercise can be done effectively in a large group or in a series of small groups, in a team meeting or in breakout sessions at a workshop.   It is a flipchart exercise, facilitated by a group member recording responses at the flipchart.

The exercise can also be enhanced by use of an overhead transparency projected as background during the flipchart responses. Use page 141 as the overhead master. If you don't use the overhead, simply read the items on p. 141 as background information to get people thinking. This information is based on the cover story in **Newsweek** magazine, June 6, 1994.

To begin the exercise, ask people to think about the descriptive stereotypes about your business/organization/ product/service that they've heard around the organization or from outsiders. Ask them to think especially about the stereotypes or descriptions that are untrue-- that is, the "media creations" about working and work at this company. Ask them also to think about the sources of these descriptions; ask them to identify the processes or persons responsible for shaping the perception. Ask them to define the internal and external "media" responsible for information and misinformation.   Give them a few minutes of thinking time, time to look at the overhead about Gen X, and then record their descriptions and comments on the flipchart(s) for discussion after all responses have been made.

If you use this as a breakout group exercise within a larger group, bring all groups back together in one large group for discussion of all comments.

139

DISCUSSION: A great deal of media hype has been generated about the so-called Generation X, the 38 million Americans in their twenties. A very good set of articles appeared in **Newsweek,** June 6, 1994. Suggest that people access it on-line for background reading, especially if your organization is populated with a staff of "twentysomethings" or their predecessors, the Baby Boomers (now in their forties, called by some "the Baboos").

The point in this series of **Newsweek** articles is that media descriptions and images often don't ring true to the facts or to the descriptions devised by the target groups and individuals themselves. In the case of Generation X, the polls and surveys by third-party pollsters are not at all true to the media creations.

This of course begs the question about what's real and what's imagined, what's motivated by the need for truth and what's motivated by the need for fiction. The Gen X story has analogies in almost every organization: dialogue on these questions helps people sort out stereotypes and biases, communication traps and alarms.

Newsweek's lead article, "Generalizations X," begins with the chilling comment, "The images baby boomers have of 20somethings are mostly unfair and untrue. It's the stereotyping of Generation X, not the reality, that bites" (6/6/94, p.61). Authors contributing to the series include: Jeff Giles, Jane Bryant Quinn, and Michael Elliott. Their ideas are combined and adapted for use in the overhead transparency master on page 141. This comment sets the tone for this exercise.

MATERIALS: Flipchart(s) and markers, overhead projector, transparency (p.141), optional copies of **Newsweek**, 6/6/94, pp.61-72.

TIME REQUIRED: 15 minutes - 1 hour.

"GENERATION X"

MEDIA CREATIONS:

Always moaning about the $4 trillion national debt

The boring twenties

Not only did they never have to fight a war, they never even had to dodge one

Unjustified, passive whining without grievance

"I hate my McJob"

In global whining, U.S. youth are Number 1

STATISTICAL REALITIES:

- Birth years 1965 - 1980, the smallest cohort since the 1950s;
  the first age group ever to be fewer in number than the group preceding it

- More young mothers in this age group are opting to stay home, out of the
  workforce, reversing a trend

- In a Roper poll, only 21 percent rated their future "very good," the lowest tally
  since 1975; entering the worst job market since World War II

- 69 percent believe that "people get ahead by their own hard work" (Roper)

- "Most people I know are trying to do things" (Katie Roiphe)

- 87 percent have a strong company loyalty (Roper)

- Have almost double the college debt ($7,000) as 1977 college graduates

adapted from Newsweek's cover story, "The Myth of Generation X", 6/6/94

42. MEET ME ON E-MAIL
from Section 3, GAMES FOR COMMUNICATION

OBJECTIVES: To formalize the communication channels possible on electronic mail; to encourage the practical-- business bottom-line-- use of e-mail.

PROCEDURE: Experiment with and then adopt a system for efficient and effective use of electronic mail within your organization. Get everyone using the system the same way in order to rid your organization forever of the obstructionists who meet for the sake of meeting and cause everyone to grumble about wasted time and irrelevant issues.

Approach this like a project or a task force assignment. Do some serious research around the organization and find out who needs to know what, how on-line personal interactions are optimally designed, and what your hardware can really do for you. Establish an "E-mail Communications R&D Project Timeline" and get on with the development and implementation of new forms of communication.

DISCUSSION: Most people like to play on e-mail. They send cryptic or humorous notes to their friends, they don't plan their "business" use of the system very well, and they generally are careless about basic principles of presentation of ideas or organization of thought in order to communicate effectively.

Change this pattern of haphazard communication to one of intentional communication, and you will have done your organization a giant favor in terms of making the power of electronic communication work for you instead of against you.

This could almost be called a game in reverse; that is, the intent of this exercise is to encourage people to stop playing games on e-mail and to use it for effective communication in today's flatter, more empowered workplace.

Bernard DeKoven of Palo Alto has available a publication "**Meeting System IQ Test**" which can be ordered via Internet at meeting@aol.com.

MATERIALS: e-mail.

TIME REQUIRED: Several days or sufficient time for an e-mail communication
                 study.

43. SECRET AGENT

from Section 3, GAMES FOR COMMUNICATION

OBJECTIVE: To use the language of spying and counterintelligence as a metaphor for scrutinizing an organization's operations to find miscommunication and misalignments.

PROCEDURE: Use an overhead projector to project the image on page 147 on a screen or wall, or use page 147 as a paper handout during a group or team meeting. This will help participants remember in a holistic way the environment of a spy operation. The "Aldrich Ames, CIA mole," case in summer 1994 will long be remembered as an important spy story in American history, triggering, perhaps, an overhaul of the entire Central Intelligence Agency (**New York Times** editorial, "One Mole, One Mountain of Trouble" on p. A20, September 28, 1994).

As in the Ames case, in business organizations too often the rules and the structure of an operation slip out of alignment with the valid mission of a company. Use the collective recollection of the Ames case to help focus people on the kinds of things that can go wrong and the fallout from these organizational disasters. Many problems arise from faulty communication, from misperception, and from a host of unwritten rules that actually determine organizational behavior. The goal here is to help people establish targets for investigation, and to identify the magnets which can draw them to the targets. Encourage creative thinking about their own organization and company as participants discuss the Ames case.

DISCUSSION: As you send people out into the organization to investigate communication and alignment problems, suggest that they consider separating out the values that motivate workers from the personal and organizational triggers that set those values in motion or that test them. Suggest that investigators use a variety of diagnosis methods, such as surveys and questionnaires; digging around the artifacts of working (what

145

people keep in their desk drawers and on bookshelves, what kinds of cartoons are posted near the copy machine, etc.); encouraging specificity in casual dialogue; interviewing people regarding the "critical incidents" that changed the course of their actions; making prioritized lists, etc.

Facilitate an internal "spy" operation to define the methods by which "surveillance" can take place and the targets of that surveillance.

Arthur D. Little Company consultant Peter Scott-Morgan has recently published a book with the appealing title **The Unwritten Rules of the Game** and the equally appealing subtitle Master Them, Shatter Them, and Break Through the Barriers to Organizational Change (New York: McGraw-Hill, 1994). His work provides excellent background reading on the general subject of communication regarding dissonance between the written rule and the unwritten rule of many a work process.

In contrast, the McBer Company, a consulting firm that has made a name for itself in the field of competency development, has a model of competencies for successful change agents. This model is presented in the December 1993 issue of **Training & Development** magazine (p. 53). This model spells out the diagnostic, interpersonal, and influencing skills a person requires to be an agent of organizational change. Worth reading too!

MATERIALS: The graphic on page 147 with memory-jogging details of the Aldrich Ames spy case.

TIME REQUIRED: Several minutes to show or distribute the graphic SECRET AGENT; 10 - 30 minutes for discussion of "spy" strategy.

SECRET AGENT

o Aldrich H. Ames, CIA
Soviet Branch Chief for European Operations

o Perceived as controversial, brazen, odd, alcoholic for years

o Exposed 34 individual agents, leading to execution of at least 10

o Flourished despite mounting suspicion, because he was a member of "the club"

o "Wherever he was, he gave away everything he had"
Senator DeConcini, Chairman of Senate Intelligence Committee

o The CIA legacy of witch hunts made it hard to conduct an effective mole hunt

o Reputed to have invented communications breaches to divert attention from
penetration investigation

o KGB gave Ames $ 2 million in exchange for "holding nothing back"

o Exposed 55 US and allied spy operations

source: New York Times
July 28, 1994 and September 28, 1994

44. SELLING VS. TELLING

from SECTION 3, GAMES FOR COMMUNICATION

OBJECTIVE: To help those on the front lines of change clearly see the difference between selling and telling as communication methods.

PROCEDURE: This is a flipchart exercise. The point of the exercise is for a group to identify steps in the action/implementation phase of driving change, and then to go back over each step and mark it with either an "S" for Selling, or a "T" for Telling, depending on which is more appropriate. The goal is to have more "S"s than "T"s because the change driver's task at the front lines of action is most often more a selling job than a telling job. If there are too many "T" ratings, go back to the drawing board and rephrase that "T" step into an "S" step.

Start the exercise by writing an "S?" and a "T?" at the top of a flipchart page. List numbers down the left margin, ready to be connected to various steps in the action phase of making change. It helps to talk in terms of a specific change that is happening or about to happen to the folks in front of the flipchart.

DISCUSSION: If people are having trouble thinking in terms of processes or steps, help them out by using an example. Here's one: "Run interference; deal with opposition and potential opposition." (This would be rated later with an "S," with the explanation that obstructionists particularly hate to be "talked to." This group, for sure, needs a "sell job" in order for their negative behaviors to begin to turn around into positive behaviors. See game 24, "Horse Trading," page 91 for one selling technique.)

A video, "The Middle Manager as Innovator" by Rosabeth Moss Kanter, is available with discussion guide from Harvard Business School Publishing Division (617) 495-6192. It is based on Dr. Kanter's lifelong study of change.

MATERIALS: Flipchart and markers.

TIME REQUIRED: 10 - 20 minutes.

45. SHIRTS
AS SUBVERSIVE ACTIVITY
from Section 3, GAMES FOR COMMUNICATION

OBJECTIVE: To provide a simple model for being an agent of change.

PROCEDURE: This is a game for one player, you, the change agent. Simply heed the admonitions reported in the November/December 1993 issue of ASTD's **National Report,** p.8. ASTD's column, "Interactive News," asked readers the question, "How do you serve as a change agent for your organization?" Selected answers from readers were published. Among the responses to the question was a simple and very much on-target response from Robert Hamilton of New Hope, Minnesota, who pointed out that good change agents are by nature "subversive." He explains that a host of small things done effortlessly and unobtrusively pay off-- things like wearing colored shirts in an organization marked by a tradition of white shirts.

Adopt this model of "shirts as subversive activity" as one kind of model for serving as a change agent. It's sometimes easier than you think!

DISCUSSION: Most formulas and recipes for being a change agent are couched in strategic language or structured flowcharts and timelines. We sometimes forget that the whole picture of a person's behavior also communicates to those around him or her. It's not only words and graphics that matter. Remember, too, that the workplace is full of right-brained types who hate formulas and flowcharts. This kind of model might just be the thing that communicates what your change is all about!

ASTD is always looking for good questions to ask readers: FAX (703)683-9203.

MATERIALS: None.

TIME REQUIRED: Several seconds of creative thinking time.

46. "SUCKER FOR A BOOK OF CIRCUITS"

from Section 3, GAMES FOR COMMUNICATION

OBJECTIVE: To use the true story of my friend, Bert, to illustrate the continued veracity of the age-old formula for effective public speaking: tell 'em what you're gonna say, tell 'em, and tell 'em what you just said.

PROCEDURE: Read or tell the story, "I'm a Sucker for a Book of Circuits," (page 155) to illustrate the point that the nature of persons on the receiving end of communication is such that they will seek, tolerate, and even need information overlap of about 30 - 40 percent in order for that communication to eventually result in changed behavior. People need the comfort of the familiar in order to learn new things.

Most storytellers embellish their stories with extra colorful adjectives and humorous or scary digressions at points during the story that are critical to the listener's understanding. If I were telling this story, I would embellish it with tales about my friend's other mechanical and technical obsessions, many of which have brought to life dramatic and delightful changes. Perhaps this story will remind you of one from your own experience that makes the same point.

DISCUSSION: Telling stories is a particular way of communicating that can bring out great truths and facilitate insight as listeners respond both emotionally and cognitively to the stories being told. This particular story is another way of helping people remember the truth in the old "how to make a speech" formula. It is also an example of how a story in a seemingly unrelated area (that is, electricity) can illustrate a point in another area (that is, communication).

Thanks to Bert Holtje, James Peter Associates, Tenafly, New Jersey.

MATERIALS: "I'm a Sucker for a Book of Circuits" story on p. 155.

TIME REQUIRED: 2 minutes for reading and uncovering the "truth" in the story.

153

"I'm a Sucker for a Book of Circuits"

I have a friend named Bert who loves to buy books on circuits--
you know, configurations of electric and electronic wires, power sources,
transformers, and such.   In fact, Bert says "I'm a sucker for a book of circuits."
Now, Bert has been buying circuit books for probably 50 years. In
adolescence, the surety that he owned a badge of belonging to the right techie
crowd-- in young adulthood, the accumulation of his very own private
expertise-- and in mid-life, the comfort of secure knowledge about circuits--
in all of these stages of life, Bert cherished his books of circuits.

Bert, to be sure, is not just a reader: he's a doer and a builder too.
Mostly, however, Bert *thinks about* books of circuits-- maybe dreams about
books of circuits. He *needs* books of circuits. He loves to know again what
he knew before, never mind that about a third of it is repetitious. Bert springs
into action easily when it comes to circuits because the wondersome
information in past circuit books just gets better with age and familiarity.   Let
him hear an old motor crank over or see an operating system flash before him
on a screen, contact a new ham radio pal in Australia for the first time, or get a
new components catalog in the mail, and he's in heaven. Bert even figured out
how to wire up a birthday greeting for me.   Bert gets all juiced up over circuits--
and he knows how to seize control of the energy that makes a difference in
learning and in life.

47. TELL ME WHAT YOU DO

from Section 3, GAMES FOR COMMUNICATION

OBJECTIVE:

To model the roving reporter style of interviewing as you try to find the best change agents in your organization.

PROCEDURE:

This "game" is built upon the ideas and techniques of competency assessment using the "critical incident" method of reporting. Imagine yourself with a roving microphone, picking out individuals who seem outstanding to interview. Imagine that you are a talk show host with an audience.

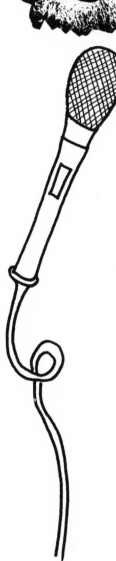

The aim of this exercise is to find out how the star performers or outstanding individuals do it. Often, they make up their own rules, they impose high standards and tough parameters on themselves, and they listen to "angel voices" unheard by most others. They accept the normal way of doing business as only the beginning, not the end, of appropriate and acceptable behavior. Through this interviewing process, you hope to find out what makes these stars shine.

Use a structured set of questions and memorize them so that you appear natural and accessible during the interview. Maintain smiling eye contact throughout the interview. When the interview is over, make notes for record about what kinds of attitudes, behaviors, knowledge, and skills are the important ones in each person. After all interviews are completed, then decide which individuals and which traits are the ones which will be useful in driving change. Use the interview as a communication tool, and the resulting communication as a planning tool.

Here are some typical questions you might ask (add your own according to your particular situation):

1.   The main question, of course, is "What does it take to be a star performer in this organization?" Or, more precisely, "Tell me what you did."

2.   Use plenty of "identify, define, describe."
        Ask "When did you personally feel most successful?"

and "What did you do at those specific times that contributed to the success?"

3.   Probe for how a person was thinking at the successful time: Ask "Will you think aloud for a minute and tell me how you analyzed the challenges of the successful action?"

4.   Probe for indicators of high levels of competency in the area of <u>control</u> or of <u>facilitation</u>. Ask "What did you do in terms of patterned behavior that always helped to get things done?"

5.   Probe for indicators of high levels of competency in the areas of <u>attitudes</u> and <u>values</u>. Ask "What motivated you to do good work?" and "What personal beliefs contributed to your success?"

6.   Ask "At what points was your influence the greatest?"

DISCUSSION: Keep the questioning focused on a critical incident, one that the person being interviewed considers a personal success. What this method tries to uncover is the "base of the iceberg," that is, the perspectives, belief systems, perceptions of self within social structures, and so on, that high performers typically have as their rock bottom. The usual analysis of knowledge and skills is supplemented by the focus on individual critical incidents and probing to describe them.

McBer and Company, Boston, pioneered in the field of competency assessment and development for business. Now Hay McBer, they can be reached for further information about critical incident and other competency assessment methods and results at (617) 437-7933.

MATERIALS: A "critical incident" interview schedule.

TIME REQUIRED: 30 minutes interviewing time per person.

48. WORTH A THOUSAND WORDS

from Section 3, GAMES FOR COMMUNICATION

OBJECTIVE: To use the power of drawing a picture to communicate a person's feeling about change.

PROCEDURE: In the early stages of an organization's experience of change, that is, several weeks after the change has been made, meet with small groups of people for a "how're we doin'?" session. Instead of direct dialogue, start off the meetings with an exercise in drawing a picture. Provide several sheets of unlined paper for each person. Simply ask them to draw a picture of how they <u>feel</u> about the change by drawing a representation of themselves at work both before the change and after the change. Suggest that they divide their paper in half, drawing the "before" picture at the top and the "after" picture at the bottom. Suggest that they may use any graphic device that comes to mind: line drawings, symbols, graphs, cartoon characters, diagrams, flowcharts, maps, etc. Encourage them to make it personal: that is, how each individual feels about the change.

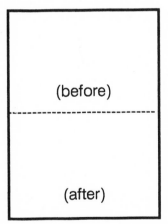

(before)

- -

(after)

DISCUSSION: After each person has drawn a picture with himself or herself in it, ask each to explain his or her drawing to the group. If people want to, have them pass around their drawings so others can see. Use the drawings as a way of communicating feelings and thoughts that are hard to put into words.

Must reading is Chapter 4, pp. 124-173 in Shoshana Zu-boff's fine book, **In the Age of the Smart Machine: The Future of Work and Power**, New York: Basic Books, 1988. The title of Chapter 4 is "Office Technology as Exile and Integration" in Part 1, "Knowledge and Computer-Mediated Work." These pages are especially important if your change has involved the "big-time" computerization of work.

Dr. Zuboff, a professor at Harvard Business School, did a major study of the effects of computerization on workers who had previously been "hands-on" kinds of workers. In her study of office workers, she additionally found that with computerization also came a loss of workers' connection with a management mentality which they previously both enjoyed and considered to be an important part of their career track. Computerization brought loss of self-esteem, irritability, short tempers, and a host of physical ailments not present in the workers' "before the change" working environment.

In her investigation, she had office workers draw before and after pictures, and did find that the picture was indeed worth a thousand words. She reproduces some of these drawings on pp. 142-149 in her book.

MATERIALS: Blank paper and pencils for drawing.

TIME REQUIRED: 15 - 30 minutes, depending on the size of the group.

49. XYZ

from Section 3, GAMES FOR COMMUNICATION

OBJECTIVE: To simplify understanding by eliminating "techie" acronyms in everyday speech.

PROCEDURE: This is a flipchart exercise to force people to see how acronym-rich and often obtuse "techie talk" impedes communication.

Take a group through a typical "dialogue day at the office" by asking them to think about and recall specifics about their own speech or the speech of colleagues that is loaded with acronyms or technical jargon. Give them a few minutes to analyze their own experience. (Bring along a particularly loaded memo that you've recently received from someone-- a memo full of acronyms and jargon. Use the memo if you have to in order to generate ideas from the group.) Ask for their ideas.

Down the left side of the flipchart page, list the acronyms or jargon phrases typically spoken around the organization. After the list has been completed, go back to the first item and ask for corrective ways of speaking. Try to get the group to think in terms of understanding and communication, rather than in terms of sounding superior or of being a member of an elite techie group. Go back over each item on the list, getting the group to define for each one a more communicative way of speaking.

DISCUSSION: Get your group to think in terms of knowledge systems or understanding systems rather than simply the usual (and technology-based) "information systems." In daily office speech, get your group to practice effective communicative speech by learning to speak without acronyms, substituting meaningful descriptive and explanatory phrases even though it might take longer. Promote technology as a people business. Talk about the values inherent in technology; for example, talk about the social and organizational human resources potential of having everyone linked together rather than talk about the advantages of "client-server architecture." Remember that technology is supposed to serve people.

Information Week magazine, June 6, 1994, in its "Final Word" column ran an interesting and helpful bit of advice from a reader, Richard A. Detweiler, president of Hartwick College in Oneonta, NY. In the column, the writer offers 10 tips on keeping technology in proper perspective as an organization grows and changes. They are abbreviated here:

1. Think both short-term and long-term at the same time, like a CEO and not like a techie.
2. Don't sell what you can't deliver. Don't sell the system's glory; sell the product that will solve the problem.
3. Think of technology as a people business.
4. Learn to speak without acronyms and technical terms.
5. Sell the philosophy of technology, not a technology philosophy.
6. Separate information and processing. Each is a separate thing.
7. Promote the company's values and mission, not technology.
8. Focus on how technology can serve people's needs.
9. Show individuals how things work. Keep it simple.
10. Don't think "I.T."; think knowledge systems.

MATERIALS: Flipchart and markers.

TIME REQUIRED: 5 - 20 minutes depending on the size of the group.

SECTION 4:
GAMES FOR ALIGNMENT

GAMES FOR ALIGNMENT
Section Overview

At this midpoint of the book **GAMES THAT DRIVE CHANGE**, the focus narrows slightly from the games in the first three sections. In this section and the two that follow it, we move from the broad scope of process, systems, and communication, to a more narrow, more directional focus in our discovery and description of change drivers. Games in this section on alignment are followed by games that focus on learning and training.

Companies and organizations of all sorts and all sizes in recent years have engaged in developing vision or mission statements that spell out "what we will become." Such targets of corporate and collective endeavor begin with the desired future state expressed in words that are value-laden and reflective of the new corporate philosophy. It is this newly worded and expressive "core" with which all organizational structures and functions seek to align. This is what alignment is all about-- it is a directional focus toward the newly defined, future-oriented, business reason for being. Alignment has to do with both personal and organizational movement toward the core, and in this pursuit, sharing the vision is a key requirement for change. The hard work of alignment is everyone's work at the individual level first, and then at the group level. The games in this section will point you in the right direction.

50. CORNERING THE MARKET
from Section 4, GAMES FOR ALIGNMENT

OBJECTIVE: To adapt the rules of play for the card game PIT (Parker
               Brothers, Beverly, MA, original copyright 1919, revised in
               1983), either figuratively or literally, to a "game" of getting the
               organizational pieces, that is, the organizational "commodi-
               ties" into alignment.

PROCEDURE: Review the play concept of the game of PIT. This is a
               traditional family card game set in the frenzy and lingo of the
               commodities exchange, complete with opening and closing
               bell. The object of the game is for any one player to corner
               the market on all nine cards of one commodity (corn, wheat,
               barley, flax, sugar, soybeans, etc.) by trading away up to four
               cards of a commodity in which his or her hand is weak.
               Shuffle, and deal nine cards to each player. An agreed-upon
               winning score is set, such as 300 points, and play proceeds
               in a lively fashion by all persons at once holding up "two! two!
               two!" or "three! three! three!" cards to get rid of on trade with
               others in the game. The concept is to trade away the bad
               stuff in order to accumulate the good stuff and get to the
               closing bell before one of the other players corners the
               market on another chosen commodity.

               If you use this game at a weekend or off-site workshop, you
               might actually purchase some games of PIT and play them in
               small groups (3 - 7 persons) so that players can catch the
               spirit of the game. Then, after a rousing game of PIT, move
               quickly into the alignment exercise which is modeled on
               gathering in the "commodity" of choice as quickly as possible,
               through negotiation.

               For the alignment game, create your own card deck similar
               to the PIT card deck. For simplicity, restrict each game to 4
               players, so that you can use a 4-item card deck of 36 cards.
               Choose an organizational alignment model (such as the
               Arthur D. Little model presented by Peter Scott-Morgan on
               page 74 of **The Unwritten Rules of the Game**, McGraw-Hill,
               1994) made up of four major sections, or create your own
               4-item model. Borrow the bell from PIT, or bring in your own.

Scott-Morgan's model suggests the four sections : stakeholders, processes, resources, and organization. Make up cards with these "suits," analogous to the PIT commodity cards. Add more interest by including a "Bull" card (for example, Tax Reform in Your Favor) and a "Bear" card (for example, Hostile Takeover). Give each suit a number of points, keeping the point spread rather small (for example, stakeholders = 50, processes = 45, resources = 40, organization = 35). Agree upon a winning score number as the object of play, such as 300 points.

Play the alignment game, "CORNERING THE MARKET," the same way you played PIT. Suggest to the players that they should try to corner the market in the area of alignment need in which they have the most ability to succeed; and conversely, they should try to get rid of the cards in alignment areas with which they have difficulty.

DISCUSSION: After the cards have been traded, have a group discussion about why a player wanted to get rid of certain cards. The game should lead you naturally into uncovering alignment problems.

If you are new to this game of organizational diagnosis, help is not far away. The field of organization development (OD) has been around for decades and has many excellent writers and thinkers in its history. Newcomers include a host of "systems" advocates who blend general systems theory with organizational studies. Look in any good business library (corporate, university, municipal) under "organization(al) development" for more ideas than you'll know what to do with! The field is full of models of organization; pick one that suits you and create your card deck around it.

MATERIALS: A deck of cards, modeled on the game PIT; the game of PIT (optional).

TIME REQUIRED: 15 minutes for play and discussion; 30 minutes to make the deck of cards.

CORNERING THE MARKET

Instructions: Make 9 cards of each suit for a game for 4 persons.

50

45

40

35

51. FILL IN THE BLANKS

from Section 4, GAMES FOR ALIGNMENT

OBJECTIVE: To compare and contrast alignment issues with a corporate mission statement in order to define which issues to work on first; to use the exercise of filling in the blanks as a way to express the alignment issues.

PROCEDURE: This is an exercise that will appeal to your left-brained analytical types who like to follow formulas and "fit the pieces together." It is an individual pencil and paper exercise to be completed in a small group setting, such as at a team or department meeting. The exercise is in two parts: (1) a fill-in-the-blank individual exercise based on each person's concerns about elements of change, and (2) a matching exercise which compares the filled in blanks with the corporate mission statement.

Create a fill-in-the-blank sheet based on the key elements of the change your organization is experiencing. Keep the number of items at about 10 -- enough to challenge one's thinking, but not so many that the exercise becomes boring. The object is to get dialogue going later about overcoming the problems in alignment. Think of items from your own particular experience and make up your own 10-item worksheet. Here are some ideas:

1. The budget for _____ is outrageous.
2. _____ is a giant waste of time.
3. Dealing with customers in the new world is _____.
4. The most effective contribution of suppliers is_____.
5. The concept of middle management should be to_____
_____.
6. Information access should be _____.
7. Discipline must be enforced in _____.
8. Training should be available to _____.
etc.

Give people a few minutes to fill in the blanks. Then ask them to read aloud their responses to the group, going around the table with all responses to item 1, then to item 2, and so on. Get all issues and concerns out on the table before going on to the matching part of the exercise. Keep dialogue to a minimum until part 2 of the exercise has been completed.

For part 2 of the exercise, distribute or project on a screen for all to see a copy of your corporate or organizational mission statement (or vision statement). Most vision statements contain the following elements:

- ☐ commitment to some truth or good
- ☐ simple statement of "we believe that..."
- ☐ clear description of mission: "therefore, we will..."
- ☐ challenges to the employees
- ☐ responsibilities of the corporation

Ask people to think about the issues raised through the fill-in-the-blank exercise in relationship to the mission statement.

DISCUSSION: At this point introduce the word "alignment" and open dialogue about where the work needs to be done in order to achieve alignment and about possible first steps in accomplishing various tasks associated with bringing the "what is" into alignment with "what should be."

Much of the language of change involves large, whole, all-encompassing movements. These are often hard for ordinary workers to grasp, especially the kinds of workers who have heretofore not had to think in terms of the "big picture." This exercise is meant to appeal to those kinds of workers-- the detail folks, those who had a pretty clear job description, and those who are used to carrying out what someone else has designed.

MATERIALS: A fill-in-the-blank sheet for each person; pencil; corporate mission statement (overhead transparency and projector).

TIME REQUIRED: 15 - 30 minutes.

52. THE FINAL FRONTIER

from Section 4, GAMES FOR ALIGNMENT

OBJECTIVES: To borrow the "trekkie" notion of space, the final frontier, in order to set people thinking about exploration of the unknown territory of living inside of corporate change. To participate in a focus group that deals with envisioning and describing their own aligned organization of the future.

PROCEDURE: This is a standard focus group and follows the typical pattern of focus group behavior: namely, facilitators are clarifiers and time managers, and participants are encouraged to suspend judgment and explore all possibilities. Advocacy of individual opinions is discouraged.

When you advertise the focus group, call it "THE FINAL FRONTIER" to begin early to get participants used to the idea of futuring. What you hope to accomplish is a creative definition of participants' own organization of the future, in perfect alignment. As the group convenes, explain the ground rules and objectives, and ask four or five key alilgn-ment questions. Use words like "What" and "What kind of" and "Which" so that you get descriptive answers, not "yes" or "no" answers. Make up your own questions, or adapt these:
1. Which organizational boundaries will be more porous?
2. What are the features of the aligned communication flow?
3. What will the CEO's monthly calendar include?
4. What will the aligned organization chart look like?
5. What corporate values must be transmitted both inside and outside of the company?

DISCUSSION: Keep discussion free flowing and involve all participants. Keep trying to get clear definitions. Save problem solving for another day.

Tom Peters is the best source of information about flexible organizations.

MATERIALS: Key futuring questions about the aligned organization.

TIME REQUIRED: About 1 hour.

53. LIVING ON THE EDGE
from Section 4, GAMES FOR ALIGNMENT

OBJECTIVE: To use the generally uncomfortable connotation of "living on the edge" as a trigger to get people to define their new roles and responsibilities resulting from organizational change.

PROCEDURE: This is a group exercise. To begin, post a "city and environs" road map of the area in which your company is located. Place the map in an area where all can see it, or clip it or tape it to a flipchart that can be brought in close to the group if they need it. Use a map that has at least 4 peripheral towns.

Use the map as a visual prop to your central theme of differentiating the center (city) core from the fringes. Get discussion going by asking the group the rhetorical question, "Where does the core end and the fringe begin?" That is, can they define where the edges of the city are-- physically, geographically, culturally, economically, psychologically? Can they agree on the definition(s)? Let the discussion flow for a few minutes as they focus on the city. When you sense that there's agreement about something, introduce the real topic of the meeting, and that is, can they agree on the core and the edges of roles and responsibilities in the new organization.   Point out that, just as in the map, the edges need definition because it's not always too comfortable being there, and surely, the more lively and vibrant core exerts a pull toward it from the edges in some key areas that define the region.

One way to make the transition from the "game" exercise of playing with the map to the real exercise of organizational role/responsibility definition is to write on the board or flipchart a list of new job titles in the changed organization. That will definitely get their attention, and help you to quickly refocus the exercise to the issue of job design for alignment.

Continue the exercise of defining the core of each new job title and of also defining its edges-- the areas of responsibility that are fuzzy or that possibly overlap another job. Stick with

175

it as long as people are thinking clearly. The outcome of the process should be agreement about the edges of jobs so that roles and responsibilities are clear in the new organization and so that the combined cores of all jobs can be aligned with each other and with the new corporate direction.

DISCUSSION: The idea is that you don't want people "living on the edge" if they are trying to align with a clear, new direction. During discussion, focus on the key issues of power, authority, privilege, territory, and accountability. Try to address these critical issues through clear job descriptions.

Writers Price Pritchett and Ron Pound, Dallas, TX, have written many helpful small books on organizational change. Their book, **Team ReConstruction: Building A High Performance Work Group During Change**, 1992, contains good advice on the people management problems during change. They make the point in this book, page 16, that without guidance in carving out clear roles and responsibilities, "employees end up carrying out a random set of duties by default, and 'organizational drift' sets in as the pathology of change." This exercise can help prevent this disaster.

MATERIALS: Road map of area (city and towns) in which you work. Flipchart and markers.

TIME REQUIRED: 30 minutes to 2 hours.

54. MBWA

from Section 4, GAMES FOR ALIGNMENT

OBJECTIVE: To learn the true nature of a company's "empowerment" of individuals through "Management By Wandering Around" (MBWA).

PROCEDURE: This is an exercise in organizational analysis using primarily the technique of listening to the pronouns that people use to talk about their jobs. It is a cursory analysis tool, popularized by U.S. Labor Secretary Robert Reich.

To do this effectively, it has to appear that you are not taking notes. Keep a tally card, a 3 x 5 index card, in your pocket so that you can record responses quickly and unobtrusively as soon as you leave a particular person. Divide the card into two columns, "they/them" and "I/we/us."

Randomly choose an interview pool. Ask only a few key questions of each person, such as, Who verifies the quality of your results? Who budgets and accounts for resources which you expend to do your job? Who decides what training you need? etc. Listen carefully as people answer your questions. Those who use plenty of "I/we/us" are probably feeling empowered; those who defer to others as the source of power (they/them) probably are not. If empowered employees are essential to alignment of work with your corporate mission, this tally will give you a pretty clear picture of where your workforce stands on the issue. Record the responses in the appropriate column to use as a basis for discussion later.

DISCUSSION: Organizations seeking alignment too often have "the name but not the game." That is, it's easy to write glowing and lofty mission statements full of worthy values; it's much harder to get employees (including top management) to demonstrate alignment by their actions and the language they use in daily interactions.

After your exercise in MBWA, organize or tally your results and present them at a group meeting attended by all who

were interviewed/observed, or write a report for your
company newsletter or to send via e-mail to all concerned.

Give feedback regarding what you discovered and its correspondence or discrepancy from the values spelled out in the
mission statement. Lead dialogue about alignment
challenges. Keep the exercise an analysis exercise.

Credit for the concept of Management By Wandering Around goes to
management guru Tom Peters, who first talked about this technique
for getting managers up from their desks and out of a bureaucratic,
paper-pushing, directive mindset in his book, **In Search of Excellence**
in collaboration with Robert Waterman (NY: Harper & Row, 1982). On
page 288 of this book, the concept was called "wandering about," and
was presented in the context of effective leadership practices.   In the
years since its introduction here, the concept and the technique has
been widely accepted as MBWA.

MATERIALS: A tally card and several key questions.

TIME REQUIRED: 1 - 2 hours.

55. MIRROR IMAGE
from Section 4, GAMES FOR ALIGNMENT

OBJECTIVE: To take a daily reading on yourself as a change driver; that is, to check yourself systematically against organizationally agreed-upon alignment tasks for leaders.

PROCEDURE: This is a game for anyone in a leadership position in a changed organization. It is an exercise in two parts: first, gather all participants together regardless of their levels of leadership for a consensus session regarding desired leadership behavior for the new company. Record the agreed-upon behaviors in list form on a flipchart. If some leadership behaviors are truly reserved for a particular leader, note that with an asterisk.

Then hand out a MIRROR IMAGE poster (page 181) to each participant. Direct their attention to the empty chart along the bottom. Ask each to copy from the flipchart onto the poster the agreed-upon behaviors in the "LEADERSHIP BEHAVIOR" column.

The second part of the game is a daily recording on the chart. The leader's job is simply to do a self-analysis each day for a specified period (for example, 3 weeks) by placing a check-mark in the box next to any behavior that the leader believes he or she has demonstrated during that working day.

Use the MIRROR IMAGE poster on page 181 as a prop for daily self-check-in sessions. If you can find it, purchase a roll of silver contact paper and cut out a "mirror" the size of the smaller oval to turn the poster into a reflecting surface. Distribute mirror posters to all leaders-- group leaders, team leaders, managers, supervisors, executives, etc. -- to post in their offices in a place where its use can't be avoided. The poster will be used daily by each leader to record his or her self-assessment for that day.

DISCUSSION: At the end of the recording period (for example, 3 weeks), reassemble all leaders for a group feedback session to talk about what was easy and what was hard. Begin to establish an honesty about alignment challenges at the leadership level. Get the point across that people want to follow leaders who know themselves and face up to their shortcomings. Facing oneself daily in a mirror is the best reminder that empowering begins with each individual, and leaders always are reflected first.

In the courageous business of change, leaders too often lose their nerve as events march onward. There are some who even advocate re-recruiting all leaders, so that those who tend to be overwhelmed by ambiguity and uncertainty are simply not "re-hired" as leaders. One way to guard against forfeiting one's leadership position is to truthfully, systematically, assess how you're doing at the new leadership. This game is a sure way to force the honesty issue.

MATERIALS: Flipchart, markers; MIRROR IMAGE poster for each leader.

TIME REQUIRED: 5 minutes at first; 1 - 2 minutes per day; about 30 minutes for discussion at the end of the self-assessment period.

MIRROR IMAGE

LEADERSHIP BEHAVIOR	DAYS	1 2 3 4 5	1 2 3 4 5	1 2 3 4 5
1.				
2.				
3.				
4.				
5.				
6.				
7.				
8.				

56. MY PLACE IN THE PROGRAM
from Section 4, GAMES FOR ALIGNMENT

OBJECTIVE: To say to someone else exactly what your personal values
               are and what kind of organization is aligned with them. That
               is, to approach the concept of alignment first from a personal
               point of view, and then to extrapolate that into an organiza-
               tional view. (Most alignment exercises are done the other way
               around.)

PROCEDURE: This is a paired exercise in which members of the pair trade
               places so that each can be both the "speaker" and the
               "coach." It is meant to be done in a large group setting, as at
               a workshop, conference, or division meeting.

               The exercise is presented on an overhead transparency to
               the large group before it breaks into pairs. The transparency
               should look something like the master on page 185 (use this
               if you can't develop you own). It should include about 25 "hot
               button" values which you've heard talked about around your
               company during the recent changes. As you project the list,
               encourage participants to add any values that they can think
               of to the list. A value doesn't have to be on the list in order
               for it to be articulated by someone during the paired part of
               the exercise. Keep the list projected during pairing.

               Be sure each person has a piece of paper or index card on
               which to make notes during discussion between pairs. The
               task is for each person to list on the card five values that he or
               she considers the core values by which he or she lives.
               Partners take turns being the "speaker" and the "coach."
               After each person has listed five, suggest that they prioritize
               them and put a star next to the top three. The person who is
               "coach" now asks his or her partner this key question: "Can
               you describe the kind of organization in which these top three
               values of yours can be lived?" Each "coach" should try to
               draw out the "speaker" so that the resulting discussion yields
               good information about alignment issues emanating from the
               individual to the company. As before, partners switch roles,
               and the other partner becomes a "coach."

DISCUSSION: The role of values and beliefs in our daily living plays a critical part in our happiness, general mental health, and individual sense of worth or self-esteem. Values by which individuals live are seldom talked about at work, and often, work values seem different and distant from individual values. In aligned organizations, however, personal values should be able to be lived out in the corporate setting.

After the paired part of the exercise, encourage participants to talk about what they learned about themselves and the organization in which they'd like to work. Focus your efforts on defining the value-based organization that is truly built upon the heart and soul of its human resource.

Two particular popular business writers in recent years have emphasized the importance of personal values in business, as well as in life. These are Peter Senge, who elaborates the idea of "personal mastery" as a critical element in building learning organizations, and Stephen Covey whose "Seven Habits of Highly Effective People" include three under a heading of "Private Victory." Both writers begin with individual values and expand these into an organizational context. Read their books for more information: Stephen Covey, **The 7 Habits of Highly Effective People**, New York: Simon & Schuster Fireside, 1989; and Peter Senge, **The Fifth Discipline**, New York: Doubleday Currency, 1990; and Senge et al., **The Fifth Discipline Fieldbook**, Doubleday Currency, 1994.

MATERIALS: An overhead transparency of suggested personal values (see page 185 as an example), projector and screen; index card for each participant.

TIME REQUIRED: 20 - 60 minutes, depending on size of the group.

achievement
challenge
community
creativity
efficiency

fame
freedom
honesty
independence
influence

intimacy
involvement
kindness
leadership
learning

love
loyalty
meaning
money
orderliness

pleasure
power
quality
respect
security

57. OUTLAWS

from Section 4, GAMES FOR ALIGNMENT

OBJECTIVES: To use the concept of the "important outsider" -- OUTLAW-- to focus on ways in which the leverage of the "outside" can move an organization faster toward alignment. To engage a small group in a building exercise using Lego™ blocks or other colored wooden or plastic children's building blocks.

PROCEDURE: Set up this exercise as a table top game for about 4 - 6 players. If your group is larger than this, break it into smaller groups of 4 - 6 persons, each group with its own table and set of blocks. The game is especially interesting if there are two or more tables of builders, so that results can be compared and discussed.

Give each table a set of blocks, with about a dozen blocks of each color, red, blue, green, yellow, white, black, for a total of approximately 72 blocks for each table. With these blocks, the team of 4 - 6 persons at each table will construct a model of the importance of "OUTLAWS" in the organization of the future.

Each team should decide which color will represent which kind of outlaw-- for example, red for customers, blue for suppliers, green for distributors, yellow for environmental standards, white for government controls such as taxes or OSHA, black for competitors, etc. Provide a pad of small sticky notes for each table in case they want to label the blocks directly.

Encourage the teams to think not in terms of the internal management structure and organization chart, but to think instead in terms of the external forces which have a heavy impact on the effective "aligned" organization of the future. Suggest that the model to be built can be a vertical tower-type model or a flat map-type model or a combination of both. The object is to work as a team and construct a representation of the interaction of the external influences on an effectively aligned organization. If you need a further representation of the internal structures of the organization, give each table a golf ball to represent the entire internal organization. What you're after is the external representation, but it sometimes helps to have an internal representation object against which to design that external model.

DISCUSSION: We have the quality movement of the last decade to thank for sensitizing us to the real bottom-line importance of involving customers and suppliers in decisions about how to run our businesses. Management guru Tom Peters talks about crossing functional barriers and dealing with porous boundaries. One sure way to see things differently is to ask for and respect those OUTLAW opinions and directives. Too often during change, we fall into the trap of talking only to our insider friends. Especially when it comes to alignment of values and business opportunities, we need also to talk to those on the outside. If these truths are not self-evident from doing the model-building at each table, remind the group of the importance of the OUTLAWS in the new world of change, networking, and global involvements. Have each group explain its model to the other group(s).

The Nobel Prize in Economics for 1994 went to three academic pioneers in the field of game theory. This was an unusual award because the theory espoused is very different mathematically from the traditional standard economic theory of "perfect competition" in which numbers are so large that no single buyer or seller ever had to worry about the response of anyone else. In game theory, however, the consequences of strategic action by one party are definitely considered by another party, and the potential and probability of reaction are intuitively and statistically figured into one's planning and economic behavior (P. Passell, "Game Theory Captures a Nobel," **NY Times**, October 12, 1994, p. D 1). This model-building OUTLAWS game can help your players realize the importance of entities/factors/people which they might never have previously considered; it can help to introduce them to new thinking about competition.

MATERIALS: Sets of building blocks and golf balls.

TIME REQUIRED: 20 - 40 minutes.

58. SUCCESS PROFILES

from Section 4, GAMES FOR ALIGNMENT

OBJECTIVES: To build a profile of success for any given job, from "the bottom up," that is, seeking and using input from any person who interacts with that particular job; to develop and validate a list of competencies that will serve the job holder in a newly aligned organization.

PROCEDURE: Do this as an individual exercise. If it is part of a workshop, allow enough time for individual work, or assign it as a pre-workshop "homework" assignment in preparation for attending the workshop. The idea is to involve as many "significant others" as possible in the defining process. Participants should include persons at all levels and pay ranges who interact with the job in question. Outsiders like suppliers, distributors, drivers, customers, etc., should also be asked to participate. The goal is to accurately and thoroughly define jobs for a changed and challenged organization.

The exercise is related to the typical job description that specifies the "essential/must have" skills and competencies, the "important to have" skills and competencies, and the "nice to have" skills and competencies. The difference here is that the company has changed, and the old job descriptions are probably out of date. This exercise is an opportunity to create the new profile of success. It features rearrangeable cards so that at any time, a new definition can be drawn based on exactly how the changes are progressing. An accurate new job description based on current competency requirements can then be developed.

First, have someone from the human resources organization make up a deck of 30 - 40 "cards" using unlined 4 x 6 index cards. There is one deck for each job being profiled.

On each card, the developer will write and briefly define a competency. Ideas can be gleaned from current job descriptions, performance review standards, needs identified in training, notations from customer complaints, hot line logs, etc. Approximately 30 to 40 different competencies or skills should be defined. The deck should also have at least 10 blank cards to encourage additional definitions.

Persons are then identified who will each get a deck of cards for the job in question-- the more variety, the more interesting the results. A deck of about 50 cards is then given to each participant with instructions to sort them into some kind of priority order that makes sense for the "new world." Suggest that there be at least 3 piles representing some kind of prioritizing or logical grouping. At some appointed time, interview the participants and codify the results into a new profile of success.

Distribute the composite profile to all participants and seek consensus or a vote on how the new job should be described.

DISCUSSION: In testing and measurement lingo, this is a creative example of an "interrater reliability study." The larger and more diverse the numbers involved, the more reliable the results can be expected to be. Use the findings for personnel decision making, including design of training programs for competency and skill development.

An interesting report of a company who did this for the position of Sales Manager can be found in **Training & Development,** September 1993, pp. 63 ff. The article, "Deck for Success," is written by Devon Scheef, TRW's Manager of Organization and Human Resource Development, Orange, CA.

MATERIALS: A deck of about 50 home-made cards for each participant.

TIME REQUIRED: 20 - 60 minutes.

59. TIN CUPPING
from Section 4, GAMES FOR ALIGNMENT

OBJECTIVE: To provide a mental model for seeking support for alignment.

PROCEDURE: Use the tin cup on page 193 as either a paper handout or overhead transparency master. Use it in group or team discussion or as a flyer to post in offices or at workstations as a reminder.

DISCUSSION: TIN CUPPING is a request-for-help technique borrowed from sidewalk beggars. In its business adaptation, it is a bargaining and negotiation tool for accumulating information, "moral" support, and financial resources-- especially money-- as one tries to line up (align) other persons and their organizations in support of one's own pet change project.

Alignment doesn't happen by dictum from on high, or even by strongly worded memos from the CEO. It happens because many people bargain and negotiate with each other during the critical first steps of implementing change "projects." Unlike "Horse Trading" (page 91, Game 24), in which there is a trade, TIN CUPPING is a one-way initiative that can only happen after a focused communication campaign directed at a specific target to "sell" a project. In TIN CUPPING, one person must ask another person for help, and say thank you. Power shifts in TIN CUPPING, and those power shifts at early implementation stages are what helps to build alignment.   It is hard to do, but often it is the only way to achieve alignment of all resources.

Chapter 6, "Empowerment," in Rosabeth Moss Kanter's classic, **The Change Masters**, New York: Touchstone, Simon & Schuster, 1984, details the case of "Chipco" managers who successfully tin cupped during important changes at their company (pp. 156ff.).

MATERIALS: The TIN CUPPING master, p. 193.

TIME REQUIRED: A few minutes.

60. UNFINISHED STORY

from Section 4, GAMES FOR ALIGNMENT

OBJECTIVES: To write an ending to a story that incorporates the writer's values and beliefs about the organization's future. To then analyze the writings for clear indications of variables -- different perspectives on personal style, motivators, work preferences, timing, etc.

PROCEDURE: Do this exercise at the beginning of a team meeting or workshop on alignment or change management. Make up your own "story beginning" from a situation or ideas that mean something to your particular organization. Several examples are included here. Type the story beginning at the top of a piece of paper leaving at least six inches of blank space for writing the ending, photocopy one for each participant, and hand them out at the start of your meeting. Encourage people to complete the page. Allow 15 - 20 minutes for story completion.

When everyone has finished, have everyone exchange papers, so that a person is not analyzing his or her own story. Before the analysis, list on a whiteboard or flipchart several key variables which the group can help to define. Use the ones listed above (Objectives) to get people thinking. Ask the group to read the endings with those variables in mind, so that you can do a tally of responses when everyone has finished the analysis. The frequency count should then lead you into a description of where your alignment problems are.

Examples of "story beginnings:"

(1)   There was once a very smart and talented young woman who was hired right out of high school as a coordinator in the company's mail room. She mastered the systems for sorting and distributing mail originating within the company complex of organizations, writing up UPS and Fed Ex tickets, and handled our managers and supervisors like a human resources pro. However, her job was in danger of disappearing when most of the company became

obsessed with e-mail and paper tickets no longer were used by carriers. After much discussion with....

(2)   Our franchisees seem to have an informal and powerful club. They have a unique view of labor-management relations that....

(3)   Target markets in the New England states are characterized by at least these three particular and important descriptors....

DISCUSSION: Encourage writers to be creative in this exercise-- suggest that they do a little "futuring" as they complete their stories. After they have finished writing, and their partners have attempted to match their expression with the items listed on the board, do a group tally by asking through show of hands who discovered this item, this item, this item, and so on. Continue discussion on each item as long as it is productive, and until you are confident that valid assessments have been made. Begin identifying projects to achieve alignment at the conclusion of this exercise.

The arena of personal style was probably defined by Myers-Briggs several decades ago. More recently, the field of Neuro-Linguistic Programming (NLP and NLP[3]) has provided other variables for dealing with analysis and definition of personal style. Look to either of these sources for more tools.

MATERIALS: A story beginning written out for each participant; whiteboard or flipchart and markers.

TIME REQUIRED: 20 - 30 minutes.

61. WHAT? HOW MANY? HOW? WHY?

from Section 4, GAMES FOR ALIGNMENT

OBJECTIVES: To identify several typical current problems in a critical area such as "job re-design" or "the path to customer service" in the newly downsized organization and to begin to design approaches to solving identified problems through the simple question test (what? how many? how? and why?)

PROCEDURE: Use this as a group exercise, best done with 4 - 6 persons who are directly responsible for making some key business processes work after a major change. It is a pencil-and-paper exercise to be done individually, with dialogue afterwards about results of the exercise.

Choose an area of the business that seems to be in shambles after a big shakeup or major organizational change. Ask participants to write this at the top of their papers, like a title of a book. This should be the same for everyone. Next, ask participants to each make three "sweeping statements" describing the top three problems in this area.

An example from the area of "job re-design" follows:
  (1) Jobs are being done by the wrong people.
  (2) Outsiders who don't care about proprietary trade secrets are doing too much of our critical and core work.
  (3) Managers are redundant and get in the way.

Now comes the real work of the exercise. Participants now must apply the four small questions at the top of this page to each sweeping statement: what? and how many? are the easiest questions and yield descriptive answers; how? and why? are the harder questions because their answers begin to explain the problem. You'll need both kinds of answers-- descriptive and explanatory-- in order to solve the problem. After about ten minutes per question, or half an hour, begin dialogue on problem solving. The goal is to establish a path of inquiry toward solving the problem. Keep the focus

197

detailed enough so that a problem-solving plan can be envisioned.

DISCUSSION: If dialogue were allowed to proceed from the "sweeping statements" phase of this exercise, a gripe session would follow. In order to be productive about problem solving, a first necessary step is for problem solvers to experience the difference between *describing* and *explaining*. This exercise using the four small questions is a quick lesson in understanding this important difference.

An interesting resource on analysis of processes affecting change is Peter Scott-Morgan's **The Unwritten Rules of the Game**, New York: McGraw- Hill, 1994, especially pp. 106 - 108. His entire book sensitizes the reader about the rules and the unwritten rules, the latter being the most important ones to fathom in order to effectively drive change. This particular exercise might uncover some of these unwritten rules; this book would be valuable reading list material for the change drivers in your group.

MATERIALS: Pencil and paper.

TIME REQUIRED: About an hour.

62. WHEEL OF FORTUNE

from Section 4, GAMES FOR ALIGNMENT

OBJECTIVES: To get out on the table different perspectives on solving alignment problems through the random selection of a spin of the wheel. To use the creative vehicle of a game of chance for the traditional "vertical conference," in order to break the typical mold of learned silence or business-as-usual generally endemic to such meetings.

PROCEDURE: This is a game for six players. These players should be from various positions, departments, or levels in an organization. They should be the same kinds of people who would normally come to a "vertical conference" of a group, division, or vice-presidential area of responsibility. The game will also work with a self-managed work team, the members of which have various types of expertise. The following people/positions might be typical:

supervisor or manager, designer/ engineer,
support staff (clerical, technical, maintenance),
salesperson, customer service representative,
information/data processing specialist.

Seat these people around a round or square table, so that they can equally participate in a game placed in the center of the table.

The game pieces consist of a deck of 12 cards (3 x 5 index cards) and a round wheel that spins. This can be made from stiff poster paper or other hard surface board such as mat board, file folder index stock, plastic sheets, etc. A pattern is included on page 201. In order to make the wheel spin, you will need two circles attached loosely together at the center with brass paper fasteners and washers. It's important that the wheel spin freely so that each player has a random and equal chance of being chosen by the spin-- that is, the good "fortune" of being selected by the game.

Divide the top circle into six equal sections and write the name of the job of each player (don't write the player's name; write the job title). Before the game begins, each player is issued two blank cards. On each card, the players are asked to state succinctly what he or she perceives to be a major alignment problem-- one problem per card. These cards will be placed face down in front of the points around the wheel, two face-down cards at each point. Some typical problems are: access to financial information, budgetary decision authority, ability to make hiring decisions, on-time distribution, knowing what's important and what isn't regarding customer complaints, communication from bottom levels to the top level, not walking the talk when it comes to support for families, etc. Make up your own list of problem areas that have a definite relationship to aligning the organizational parts. The object of the game is for the player who spins the wheel to tell how he or she would solve the alignment problem on the turned-over card ***if he/she were the person indicated by the random spin.***

Play begins with one person who both spins the wheel and turns over the top card in front of him/her. Suppose that the sales rep turns over her card which says "ability to make hiring decisions." She spins the wheel and when it stops, the point in front of her face-up card says "support staff." She then must tell how she (actually the sales rep) would solve this problem if she were the support staff person. She might say something like, "Well, I really need some training first in how to conduct an interview in today's diversity-conscious world" or "I really don't ever want to make hiring decisions because I'm scared to death of the law and would quit my job here if I had to do that." At the end of play, the turned-up card is placed face up under the other card. Continue around the table in a clockwise fashion until all cards have been turned up and all players have responded.

DISCUSSION: What happened here is a doubly different perspective on an alignment problem, "forced" by the nature of the game.

This game is also good for helping people see various "mental models" of the sort talked about by Peter Senge in his books on the learning organization.

MATERIALS: 12 index cards and a WHEEL OF FORTUNE (p. 201).

TIME REQUIRED: About 1 hour.

WHEEL OF FORTUNE
<u>Note to user:</u> Enlarge this template on an office copier before working on it.

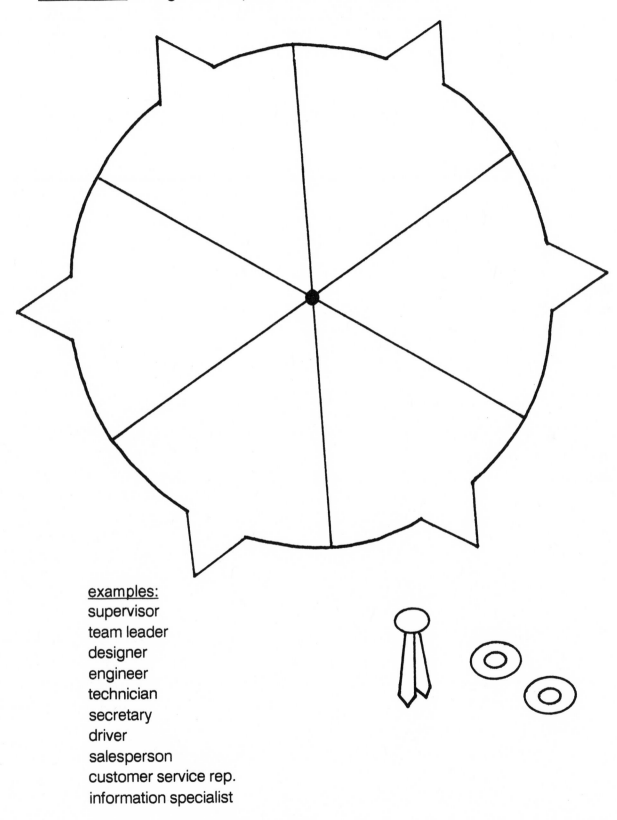

<u>examples:</u>
supervisor
team leader
designer
engineer
technician
secretary
driver
salesperson
customer service rep.
information specialist

63. YOU GOTTA BE KIDDING!

from Section 4, GAMES FOR ALIGNMENT

OBJECTIVE: To "break the ice" at a new team or group meeting by having participants sit behind a specific tent card with which they identify in some way.

PROCEDURE: Prior to the meeting (to talk about issues in alignment), make name cards like one typically finds in vendors' seminars. Make your own by folding a large index card in half so that both sides of the "tent" can contain a slogan. Make about 20 percent more cards than you need (for example, 12 cards for 10 people), so that all persons have a choice of where to sit. Write the same slogan on both sides of the tent card prior to the meeting. This is so that the other persons around the table can see each person's slogan of choice.

Choose slogans that are similar expletives to "You Gotta Be Kidding!"-- that is, dredge up from your memory all of those killer comments people typically have made around your organization that deep down indicate some insecurity about implementing change. Here are some for starters: "Too political," "Too structured," "Too loose," "What a waste," "Too simple," "Too complicated," "All fluff and no stuff," "Too theoretical," "Absolutely impractical," "No way," "Yes, but..."

Place one tent card on the table in front of each chair. As participants enter the room for the meeting, ask them to please find a seat behind a slogan that has some meaning to them.

DISCUSSION: After everyone has found a seat, suggest that these surly slogans and killer comments are really subtle signals that the user of such a comment is about to learn something new. Each invites further explanation; most indicate a strong opinion about how things _should_ work.

Icebreakers are traditional props in the trainer's theater. This one is especially useful in setting the stage for dialogue about alignment.

MATERIALS: Tent cards, surly slogans, and killer comments.

TIME REQUIRED: 3 minutes.

64. YOU'RE ON CANDID CAMERA!
from Section 4, GAMES FOR ALIGNMENT

OBJECTIVE: To view videotapes of monthly directors' or officers' meetings in order to identify alignment issues of importance to the company's leaders.

PROCEDURE: Show videotapes to small work groups or teams who will systematically analyze the board meeting for alignment issues. Do this regularly, for example, every month for six months, until you feel that the organization is truly in charge of the change and working toward alignment.

Design a viewer's checklist or matrix of some sort to guide the viewing in a systematic way. One type of thing might be to simply answer two basic questions: (1) What are the "good words" favored by participants at the board meeting? (list the words or phrases), and (2) What are the "hot buttons" evident in discussions at the board meeting? (list or describe the things that always cause a reaction in another participant). The simplest form of matrix is made by drawing a single line down the center of a piece of paper, labeling one column "GOOD WORDS" and the other column "HOT BUTTONS." As group/team members view the tapes, ask them to look and listen carefully for possible entries in each column. Ask them to write down what they observe.

DISCUSSION: During discussion after the tapes, talk about whether or not the group's alignment issues are the same as those evidenced by the board meeting's good words and hot buttons. Help the group sort out what's important and what isn't important in alignment deliberations and planning.

> One of the key elements in the psychology of individual empowerment is the idea of access to necessary and sufficient information. This exercise helps individuals identify what information they need in order to work toward alignment.

MATERIALS: Videotapes of regular board of directors' meetings; matrix.

TIME REQUIRED: 1 - 2 hours.

SECTION 5:
GAMES FOR CONTINUOUS LEARNING

GAMES FOR CONTINUOUS LEARNING
Section Overview

Whatever your definition of the learning organization is, it probably includes the idea that in order to achieve it, the people and the organizational processes themselves must be capable of and practitioners of continuous learning. We know that, given the right motivation and tools that fit, most people can become learners. We also have generally come to believe that organizations can also learn, and that often the learned organizational whole is greater than the sum of its learning parts. We say that in business today we want people who can think across a range of topics and technologies, who are flexible and adaptable, and who are turned-on to investing in their careers through learning. We believe that learning can accrue to provide a company with a competitive edge, that systems and practices can be fashioned to support learning, and that good results such as customer satisfaction and bigger market share often come from organizations where continuous learning has been a vision and a reality. Games in this section will help you become continuous learners.

65. THE CHALLENGE
from Section 5, GAMES FOR CONTINUOUS LEARNING

OBJECTIVE: To encourage participants to list the challenges of being able to continuously learn on the job, through the metaphor of the bullfight.

PROCEDURE: This is a flipchart exercise which works well as a breakout room exercise as part of a larger conference on becoming a learning organization. In this situation, each breakout room group gathers around a flipchart in the breakout room, and all groups report back to the main reassembled group when the exercise is complete. It can also be used with a small group at a single flipchart.

Use the pattern on page 213, representing the bullfighter's cape and re-draw it in red marker on each flipchart. Fill the chart with the cape; make it spacious enough to write the identified "challenges" inside. The imagery of the "fight" should help the creative juices flow as participants list the learning challenges. Fill in the capes with a color other than red.

DISCUSSION: Discussion will be richer if each breakout room considers a different type of challenge. Write a different challenge category on each flipchart and suggest that the group in that room stick to listing challenges related to that category. Here are some suggestions of challenge categories:

- ☐ invention
- ☐ intentional reflection
- ☐ rewarded risk taking
- ☐ assessment of organizational learning capacity
- ☐ sharing individual expertise with each other
- ☐ mapping personal learning needs
- ☐ identifying systems that don't work
- ☐ explaining systems that do work
- ☐ setting up the learning environment.

In order to prevent sincere efforts at becoming a learning organization from being just so many good words, you'll need detailed, focused exercises to get people to think clearly about specifics-- who, what, when, where, how many, how, and why. Like any other kind of system assessment or up-front analysis, the system which must be in place to support continuous learning must be seen as a sum of parts-- analyze, design, develop, evaluate; plan, do, check, act; reflect, generate; etc. This exercise helps you look carefully at parts.

MATERIALS: A flipchart and markers for each breakout room; the pattern of a matador cape (p. 213) to copy onto each flipchart.

TIME REQUIRED: 20 - 30 minutes plus discussion time in the reassembled group.

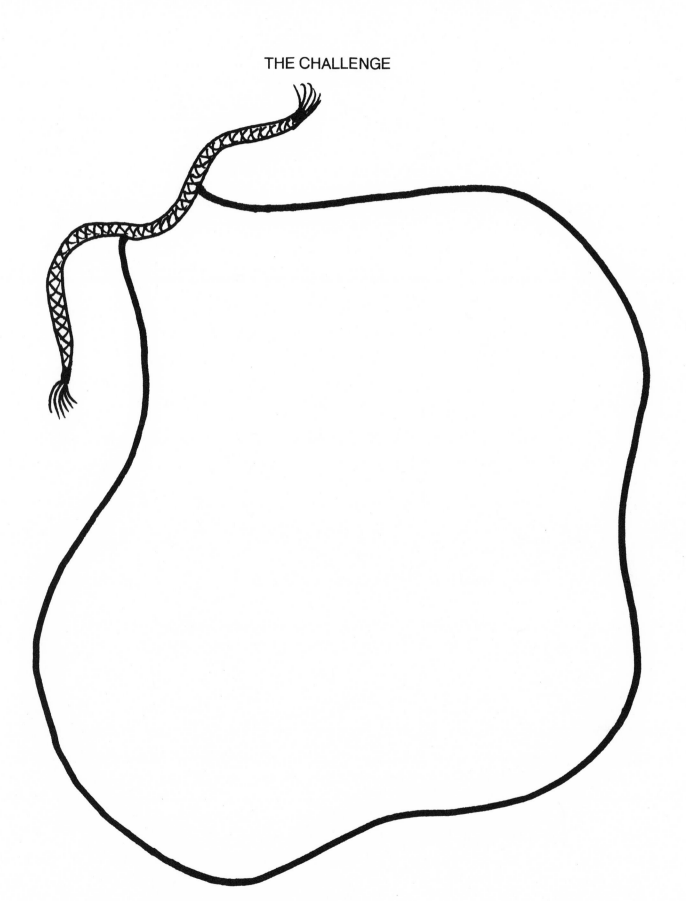

67. CYBERSTAGES AND OD
from Section 5, GAMES FOR CONTINUOUS LEARNING

OBJECTIVE: To use the analogy of learning one's way around an on-line computer service (America Online, CompuServe, Internet, etc.) to identify the processes needed for becoming a learning organization.

PROCEDURE: By now, most organizations have a group of employees who have experimented with an on-line service, either as parents of adolescents who hang out in chat rooms or as alumni/ae of cyberspace exploration themselves. The memory of that kind of experiential learning will be fresh in the minds of such explorers. This exercise makes use of that fresh memory.

Use this exercise as an icebreaker or point of focus at the beginning of a planning session. Use a flipchart or whiteboard if you want to record responses; otherwise, simply do it as a verbal exercise to get the ideas flowing.

As participants gather, casually chat about their on-line services and encourage them to share stories; engage in informal dialogue about their or their families' experiences with e-mail, chat rooms, bulletin boards, lobbies, flaming, and other features of their electronic worlds. Keep the free-flowing exchange going until everyone is involved actively as an initiator or responder.

Then shift from informal to formal inquiry. If there are a number of people in your group who have children at home who've been on-line for a while, direct your initial questioning to them. Ask them to think about the stages of growth which their kids have gone through. Ask them to specify the programs or games they've played. Ask them to label or identify at least three stages. Expect answers something like: The Who Dunnit Stage, The Search and Destroy Stage, The Intergalactic Adventure Stage, The Tiptoe Around the Internet Stage, The Look for Trouble Stage, The Finding Cool Information Stage, The I'm In Control Here Stage, etc. (Most participants can find parallels in their own growth stages with those of children on-line.)

After the stages have been identified, get some sort of consensus about the best hierarchical order in which to organize them. Then shift focus once more. This time, ask participants to use the analogy of the "cyberspace stages" of growth to their organization's stages of growth in becoming a learning organization. Ask them to now identify and define the stages of growth which will have continuous learning of various sorts as a key characteristic. Suggest that both personal and individual stages as well as organizational or corporate stages are desired. Then, as before, get general consensus on the hierarchy of these organizational developmental stages of growth.

DISCUSSION: This exercise can be a lot of fun especially if your 30-somethings and 40-somethings in the group have children who are turned-on to America Online or CompuServe and have gotten through to the Internet. A very "present" kind of learning happens when individuals experiment with communication into literally new ways of talking, writing, responding, and handling conflict on-line. The memory of such experiential exploration is fresh, and can be tapped to bring innovation, creativity, and enthusiasm to organizational analysis which would otherwise seem dull.

Theoretical background for stage theory of growth is rich and widely accepted. Leaders in the field have included Piaget, Bruner, Erickson, and Kohlberg. Likewise, the field of cognitive studies contributes to the notion that some things need to be learned before other things can be learned, and that upward movement through stages is best done gradually and systematically. The work of Bloom is fundamental here. Education libraries will contain many references to all of these thinkers.

MATERIALS: Flipchart or whiteboard and markers.

TIME REQUIRED: 15 - 30 minutes.

67. DOODLES
from Section 5, GAMES FOR CONTINUOUS LEARNING

OBJECTIVES: To make one's work space more creative by playing in small ways in it. To use small periods of play as a reminder that sport, games, and joyfulness often open up the scene to possibilities for new kinds of learning.

PROCEDURE: Encourage employees to find ways to play in small ways. Here are some ideas: doodle with fluorescent markers, play wastebasket basketball, use a kaleidoscope while talking on the telephone, rearrange your bookcase so that a Slinky™ can walk over your horizontally stacked books from time to time, have races with wind-up toys, make paperclip chains and designs using a magnet. Encourage play at any time.

DISCUSSION: Play is a diversion from the ordinary left-brain, logical, analytical way in which we do most of our work. Play relieves stress, rejuvenates us, and opens our thinking to creative connections we might not otherwise have considered. Think of play not as a waste of time, but, rather, as an exercise of your right brain.

Continuous play can lead to continuous learning of the right-brain type: spatial, intuitive, divergent, sensuous, imaginative, abstract, and impulsive. Creativity and innovation are in great need of re-discovery in American workplaces. "Doodles" can help!

MATERIALS: Toys of choice that fit easily into workstations or offices.

TIME REQUIRED: A few seconds whenever the spirit moves.

217

68. DOWN WITH "PIZZA, PADS, AND PILLS"!

from Section 5, GAMES FOR CONTINUOUS LEARNING

OBJECTIVE: To use the case study of Astra/Merck in re-designed pharmaceutical sales strategies as an example of continuous learning applied to bottom-line business.

PROCEDURE: Reproduce copies of George Harrar's excellent case study article, "Pills 'n' Pads No More," in **Forbes ASAP**, June 6, 1994, pp. 36-42. Distribute these to your team or group for study prior to a group meeting on continuous learning or building a learning organization. Ask your readers to list at least three important ideas about CONTINUOUS LEARNING in this article.

DISCUSSION: Set a meeting time and ask people to come with their ideas and to be ready to discuss learning strategies for your own organization/company that might borrow from Astra/Merck's way of thinking.

The essence of the change was that Merck's new sales strategy would be tied to a salesperson's 486 XE laptop computer loaded with Lotus Notes 3.0 rather than the freebie pills, personalized note pads, and lunchtime pizza which have been the salesperson's stock in trade for many decades. A menu including up-to-the-minute clinical studies, drug fact sheets, literature searches, and a host of patient and client information could be instantly personalized to a particular physician's or HMO administrator's needs. Information and continuous learning are seen as the competitive advantage in this new way of doing business.

> Merck calls this selling drugs with information, not with trinkets. It's worth reading about!

MATERIALS: Copies of the article referenced above.

TIME REQUIRED: 20 minutes for reading and making notes.

69. FORK IN THE ROAD
from Section 5, GAMES FOR CONTINUOUS LEARNING

OBJECTIVE: To use Robert Frost's famous poem, "The Road Not Taken,"
               as a source of images and ideas regarding action and
               reflection, reality and imagination.

PROCEDURE: Photocopy the poem found on page 223 for each member of
               your group or team. Read the poem aloud, or have a group
               member who's good at such things read the poem aloud to
               the group as each person follows along on his/her copy.
               Before reading begins, suggest that each person notice
               Frost's way of saying things, and perhaps highlight phrases
               of particular beauty or significance.

               After the reading, ask participants to identify a problem or
               decision point which diverges in two directions, like Frost's
               two roads in the woods.

DISCUSSION: Facilitate a discussion of alternatives, referring back to the
               poetic expression of the poem. Encourage participants to
               elaborate on their feelings such as "sorry I could not travel
               both" or "knowing how way leads on to way" or keeping "the
               first for another day." Continue discussion until someone
               says something like "What if we take the road less traveled?"
               It's the "what if" question that will lead you into seeing the
               possibilities for learning-- and even for continuous learning.

Milan Moravec, a management consultant of Walnut Creek, CA, in
Information Week, June 27, 1994, p. 92, said that the appropriate attitude
to start with in managing change such as downsizing is "that downsizing is
a fork in the road." He further states that it is a transition to be managed
with insight, innovation, and compassion -- poetic language, indeed. It's
worth revisiting Robert Frost, especially at times characterized by "forks."

MATERIALS: A copy of Frost's poem, "The Road Not Taken," p. 223.

TIME REQUIRED: 5 - 15 minutes.

The Road Not Taken
by
Robert Frost

Two roads diverged in a yellow wood,
And sorry I could not travel both
And be one traveler, long I stood
And looked down one as far as I could
To where it bent in the undergrowth;

Then took the other, as just as fair,
And having perhaps the better claim,
Because it was grassy and wanted wear;
Though as for that the passing there
Had worn them really about the same.

And both that morning equally lay
In leaves no step had trodden black.
Oh, I kept the first for another day!
Yet knowing how way leads on to way,
I doubted if I should ever come back.

I shall be telling this with a sigh
Somewhere ages and ages hence:
Two roads diverged in a wood, and I--
I took the one less traveled by,
And that has made all the difference.

from *THE POETRY OF ROBERT FROST*
edited by Edward Connery Lathem

70. 4 FACES OF HAL

from Section 5, GAMES FOR CONTINUOUS LEARNING

OBJECTIVE: To use the film hero HAL, the supercomputer from the futuristic film <u>2001: A Space Odyssey</u>, as a reminder of the many kinds of learning the "future" employee will have to demonstrate.

PROCEDURE: Rent or purchase the video <u>2001: A Space Odyssey</u> and have your team/group view it. As they are watching, suggest that they make notes about the various kinds of learning that HAL uses. Here are some clues: controls flight, monitors life-support systems including using feedback, plays chess, psychoanalyzes the crew, converses in English. Viewers' notes can be a simple list of items such as these, or they can be elaborations about the nature of the learnings which HAL demonstrates. After the film, group the viewers' responses into logical categories and name each category. Try to name at least four different categories.

HAL, the computer, is a continuous learner. Real-life viewers can be helped to see what kinds of learning are necessary to intelligent and purposeful existence in their own future. Record the categories with entries under each heading on a flipchart or whiteboard. Use this exercise at the beginning of a design meeting on instructional systems, personal goal-setting, or organizational visioning.

DISCUSSION: Help people to see HAL as a tutor, kindly mentor, an investigative partner, an intelligent tool. Help people to see that they, too, need to adopt these kinds of learning postures. Help people to see that they must be able to generate ideas; manage, move, and classify information; make assessments and judgments; define and solve problems.

In the mid-1970s, many projects were launched in the field of Artificial Intelligence, spurred on by futuristic characters such as HAL. **IEEE Transactions on Systems, Man, and Cybernetics**, May 1975, contains many fascinating reports and papers, among them "Four Faces of HAL," pp. 375-380.

MATERIALS: A videotape of the movie <u>2001: A SPACE ODYSSEY</u>,
               flipchart or whiteboard and markers.

TIME REQUIRED: 2 hours.

71. I WOULD LIKE TO...

from Section 5, GAMES FOR CONTINUOUS LEARNING

OBJECTIVES: To use the direct approach to employees by simply asking them what they would like to do-- to learn, to change, to be happy, to be successful, etc. To listen to employees.

PROCEDURE: Call a meeting for the specific purpose of listening to what employees have to say. Make it clear that each person must speak up, and that each will be heard. Simply ask each person directly, "What would you like to learn?" Save other types of wish lists for other meetings-- one meeting devoted to one topic only. Keep listening until each person has finished his or her wish list of learning, no matter how long or short it is. You'll be amazed at what you all will learn.

DISCUSSION: This exercise should need no prompting, but it probably does. Most companies are used to a style of change management that is driven by the top; that is, memos, directives, and policy statements coming out of the executive office or board of directors somehow are expected to be implemented without a hitch by everyone below. "Do it because I say so and I'm the boss" has been a way of doing business for decades. Empowerment, innovation, and change of culture happen first and best, however, because of individual awakening and habitual action.

To be a good active listener, keep in mind that you are the receiver, not the initiator of the idea. Get yourself in the frame of mind to accept what you are hearing without making judgmental remarks at the time. If you don't understand something you are hearing, ask for clarification or elaboration. "Say more" is a good thing to say if you aren't sure you got the message. The good listener keeps an open mind and thinks expansively. Think about how to do this before the meeting; get your head set correctly. Save acting upon what you hear for another kind of meeting at another time.

MATERIALS: None.

TIME REQUIRED: Several minutes per person.

227

72. IN THE MEANTIME
from Section 5, GAMES FOR CONTINUOUS LEARNING

OBJECTIVE: To develop a corporate "game" -- that is, an innovative support mechanism for the honorable employee who gets downsized out of a job.

PROCEDURE: This is a task for managers who have had to terminate employees because of re-engineering or downsizing. The idea is to think very creatively about the ways in which these individuals will handle their employment future "IN THE MEANTIME." Finding psychologically, socially, and economically valuable things to do between periods of employment should and could be a new mandate of the worker in partnership with the employer he/she is leaving. Managers can do a whole lot to help set up "the meantime" for the general benefit of a shared prosperity that Americans desire. The idea of continuous learning is a captivating one, and one which could drive the kinds of change required to deal effectively with the problem of "the meantime."

Being fortified with the proper mindset is the first task. The next task is to devise and set in motion a program of support. This kind of thing is made to order for regional group sponsorship, Chambers of Commerce, industry consortia, community colleges, and other voluntary associations of businesses. The first step is articulating the will to act.

DISCUSSION: At the heart of the economics of downsizing and re-engineer-ing is the paradox between resulting higher productivity across the board and accrued lost wages, resulting perhaps in not a net gain for society as a whole. Those in leadership positions, who make bottom-line decisions, must think in terms of the whole employment picture and the people who want to or have to work for a living. Simply helping folks write a new resume is not the answer; something related to continuous learning is. If you can think creatively, as if you were designing a game-- one that required different perspectives, strategic thinking, motivation to enter, and space for all to play-- you'll have a better chance of overcoming the fears and negative thinking that typically accompany major change and instability.

Robert Kuttner of the **Washington Post** Writers Group, in an article reprinted in **The Berkshire Eagle** newspaper (August 1, 1993, p. E1) after the Chicago conference on jobs, reported the use of the term "new social contracts" for the workplace. President Bill Clinton moderated the high-level conference co-sponsored by the Departments of Labor and Commerce called, "Workplace of the Future."

While it is true that some downsized employees can and want to become entrepreneurs, plying their skills with ease in a boundary-less workplace over electronic paths and highways, the majority of those "in the meantime" do not have anything meaningful to do, from the perspective of recognized and legitimized economic contribution. Kuttner's article suggests that the reality of shed jobs requires new public policy initiatives such as fringe benefits like child care, health insurance, pension, and re-training becoming "perquisites of citizenship," not of employment in a particular job. He calls for "better buffers" for folks between jobs, calling on employers and government to "devise something better for workers between jobs than unemployment compensation."

MATERIALS: None.

TIME REQUIRED: As long as it takes to think creatively.

73. INTENTIONAL READING

from Section 5, GAMES FOR CONTINUOUS LEARNING

OBJECTIVES: To engage in intentional reading of several important corporate documents in order to identify one's information processing style(s). To become intentional about reading as a tool for continuous learning.

PROCEDURE: Do this exercise in pairs. It is an exercise in document analysis according to a prescribed template, found on page 233. This kind of reading is a tool both for document analysis in general and for self-analysis regarding learning to learn. Each reader is expected to complete a TABULATION OF INTENTIONAL READING chart (p. 233). Have a copy of the blank chart for each participant.

Begin the exercise by distributing a copy of several important short documents to be analyzed, for example, the corporate mission/vision statement, the list of quality principles, a recent article about the company in a newspaper, etc. The exercise is to be done individually and silently. Have highlighter markers and pencils available for participants.

The first task is for each person to read each document carefully. Instruct participants to then skim back over the document, and, using the highlighter or pencil, cue the <u>next</u> reader of the document (the partner) about the important words or phrases. Then, have the pairs switch marked documents. The point of the exercise is for the second reader, the reader of the cued document, to use the chart for analysis of himself/herself regarding the next steps of learning, namely, how information was processed and made useful after cueing. Most people never give any thought to how they read-- but in order to get ready to become a continuous learner, reading tools are among the first essentials in one's learning toolbox.

To use the chart (p. 233), participants probably will need a few minutes of explanation of the three categories across the top: Rehearse, Integrate, and Construct. Take the time to define these and clarify them if people have questions. Readers will copy each cued element into the appropriate column, indicating how they actually "read" that cue, that is, how that cue was processed by that second reader.

DISCUSSION: <u>Rehearse</u> means that when you see a cued term, for example, the word *Baldrige*, you would say it over and over again to yourself in order to get it in your head that there is no letter "d" after the letter "i" in its second syllable. You might even spell it over and over again until you were sure you had it right.

<u>Integrate</u> means relating the cued word or phrase to something already in your memory, for example, if the phrase *corporate responsibility* were highlighted, you might think of the company's benefit package which employees enjoy, or you might recall a magazine article you read about another particularly responsible corporation. You might attempt to compare/contrast those elements about corporate responsibility already in your memory with this cued item in your company's mission statement.

<u>Construct</u> means that you take the cued element and apply imagination to it, constructing or building it into some other, perhaps logically unrelated idea. For example, you might find the word *environment* highlighted, and you might admit to yourself that you hate this green movement around the world, so that every time you see that word in company documents from now on, you will replace it in your mind with the image of a red stop sign.

Helping employees develop the tools they'll need for continuous learning is the hard part of becoming a learning organization. This exercise is one way to combine the "good words" of key corporate documents with a real self-help tool. Intentional reading and intentional learning double the punch!

MATERIALS: A TABULATION OF INTENTIONAL READING chart for each participant, highlighter pens, pencils; several important short corporate documents.

TIME REQUIRED: About an hour.

TABULATION OF INTENTIONAL READING

Rehearse	Integrate	Construct

Other styles or comments:_____

_____

_____

74. IVD

from Section 5, GAMES FOR CONTINUOUS LEARNING

OBJECTIVES: To "get inside the head" of an interactive videodisc (IVD) designer by imagining the development process necessary to produce a teaching-learning IVD; to simulate the design process, paying special attention to the generation of alternative paths through information. To use this as a model for problem solving and continuous learning.

PROCEDURE: Choose a typical business scenario in which key decision points can be easily seen, for example, a salesperson's "prospecting" via telephone, or the customer-salesperson relationship during closing the sale, or the engineer-salesperson relationship regarding description of product features, etc. Describe this scenario to your group/team as an "icebreaker" for a planning meeting.

To begin, ask for help from two people in your group. After you describe the scenario, ask the two "volunteers" to talk to each other-- not role play, just dialogue-- about what they each understand as the important elements of the process each side must go through in order to make progress. Use this dialogue to simply get ideas out on the table; welcome any comments from the others in the group. Use this modified brainstorming technique to stimulate the production of ideas on a specific subject. Get a general agreement that the process articulated by the two is how it usually works. Then have them return to being just a part of the group.

Now the central simulation task is given to all present. Give a time limit, such as 15 minutes, by which each person should list the key decision points in the scenario. These must be places in the development of the sale (or other topic) where the choice of action or decision will have a great effect, one way or the other, on the business. Suggest that each person try to list at least 5 such key decision points. When all have finished listing, write their ideas on a flipchart in some kind of logical order.

235

DISCUSSION: Then go through each item and ask "What if this was the decision here?" Can you think of any other appropriate or inappropriate action? (Remember the old flowcharts programmers always had to draw?--- This is a similar exercise.) The metaphor of the IVD can help stimulate people to think like they were interacting with a computer and CRT, like they were playing a sales simulation computer game. Designers of IVD simulations have to think in terms of options, alternative paths, and plausible choices. These are all important in the search for ways to think like continuous learners. The skills need to be practiced. This is one way to do it without having to buy the expensive IVD training program.

Teaching employees to be aware of how they think is a fascinating and important job. Exercises like this one can be very helpful as a model for problem solving and learning.

MATERIALS: Pencil and paper; flipchart and markers.

TIME REQUIRED: 30 minutes.

75. THE Nth DEGREE
from Section 5, GAMES FOR CONTINUOUS LEARNING

OBJECTIVES: To use principles and practices of creative thinking applied to problems that surfaced because of a major change; to identify how continuous learning can be part of the solutions.

PROCEDURE: This "game" is good as an energizer directly after lunch or around 3 p.m. at a workshop session. As people reassemble, write on a flipchart or whiteboard the terms **Nth, X^3,** and **Y^2.** Draw a bell curve with long tails going out to at least six sigma. Use different colors for each item. When folks see these, they'll mutter or giggle nervously and get in exactly the right frame of mind for the exercise!

When everyone has arrived and is seated, ask the group to state three obvious problems that were "caused" by the recent change. Expect responses such as: no clear job descriptions, too few sales reps for the customer base, impossible expectation that everyone will be able to use PCs and laptops, glitches in distribution because of reduced staff, equipment maintenance problems because no one's in charge, etc. Write these down on the whiteboard or on another flipchart (I prefer to use two flipcharts for this exercise).   "Number" each one with a letter, A, D, K, N, J, X-- choose a letter that is prominent in the problem statement such as "J" for "no clear job descriptions." Keep an element of surprise in this game.

Next, tell the group that they're going to apply some creative problem-solving techniques to these problems. Choose one of the problems and ask everyone to focus for a minute only on that one. Call it by its letter, "Problem N," for example. Read this list of words to the group:
          add, subtract, multiply, divide;
          combine, substitute, raise to the power of, reverse.
Ask the group to consider applying one or more of these terms to Problem N. For example, Problem N might be no one to answer the phones. Ask, What can we <u>add</u> to solve this problem, making the solution an "N +" solution? Or

ask, What can we <u>substitute</u> for phones? Keep discussion going as long as it is productive-- encourage seemingly outrageous responses; this can be an amazingly energizing endeavor and can produce astounding results.

DISCUSSION: These are all mathematical terms used to manipulate numbers; the concepts inherent in these terms can be used to think more creatively about words and problem situations. In our workplaces, we have not typically been encouraged to think this way; we've been acculturated to separate work from fun, and have overemphasized the left-brain way of doing things. Using these math concepts neatly bridges the gap between problem-solving approaches and is usually easy for participants.

Wonderful examples of companies who have used these kinds of creative problem-solving techniques are beginning to show up in human resources literature. Probably the most famous example is Baldrige Award winner Motorola whose concept of total quality management by using the goal of "Six Sigma" measurement transformed the corporation. Other examples are described in a new publication by Michael Michalko, a card deck called **Thinkpak**, Berkeley, Ten Speed Press, 1994. The instruction book is particularly good.

MATERIALS: Two flipcharts and a set of colored markers.

TIME REQUIRED: 10 - 20 minutes.

76. OPERATIVE

from Section 5, GAMES FOR CONTINUOUS LEARNING

OBJECTIVE: To create one's own board game of the path to continuous learning.

PROCEDURE: Use this mind-bending exercise in a meeting or workshop which has gotten boring with too much "dumped" information, or simply as a break from a group session heavy in procedure or methodology. This exercise gets at "process" by a different route.

The aim of the exercise is for each person to make up his or her own board game. There are five rules or constraints which must be obeyed during the design of the game:

1. There must be a start to the game.
2. There must be a finish to the game.
3. There must be 2 <u>Trap</u>s defined, between start and finish that impede progress.
4. There must be 2 <u>Fortunate Find</u>s defined, between start and finish that spur progress forward.
5. There must be 4 <u>Stops Along the Way</u> for gaining information, giving information, making important contacts, solving sub-problems, etc.

Symbols may be used to make the game board look like a real game board (Monopoly, Parcheesi, or Candyland, etc.) and to stimulate creative, holistic thinking: a diamond shaped caution sign for a Trap, a rainbow for a Fortunate Find, and an octagonal stop sign for a Stop Along the Way. Each person must develop his or her game independently, and may choose any topic from among these (or any other of particular importance to your own company):

☐ Creating a vision
☐ Providing executive support
☐ Developing management systems
☐ Maintaining information flow
☐ Designing jobs
☐ Working in teams
☐ Working alone
☐ Earning rewards

239

The game title may be any of these chosen bullet items or some clever title referring to the chosen topic. The challenge is: By what path must I operate in order to be a *continuous learner* regarding_ _ _ _ _ _ (one of the above)? The game should be designed to answer this question and get from start to finish following the five rules for game design. The path may be circuitous, winding, straight, or any configuration at all.

Give each person a copy of the game board layout on p. 241. This can be used directly, or just the gameboard part of it may be copied to another larger piece of paper. Share results when everyone has finished. Traps, Fortunate Finds, and Stops should be labeled.

DISCUSSION: This game is meant to encourage creative thinking, with elements of both initiating action and engaging in reflection. Through the concreteness of drawing the path from start to finish, participants should be helped to see the benefit of making choices about what's important in "process" design. The game should help people see the value of planning, moving forward, and looking behind and to the sides for possibilities for both positive and negative influences.

Most of us as we go from being a "sometimes" learner to being a continuous learner need to be reminded that it's necessary to make intentional choices about elements of the processes along the path to solving problems. Building a learning organization requires independent and creative approaches from many people working together toward the same finish line.

MATERIALS: A game board layout for each person (p. 241). Enlarge this on an office copy machine if you want it bigger.

TIME REQUIRED: About 1 hour.

Game Title:

Choose one :
- ☐ Creating a vision
- ☐ Providing executive support
- ☐ Developing management systems
- ☐ Maintaining information flow
- ☐ Designing jobs
- ☐ Working in teams
- ☐ Working alone
- ☐ Earning rewards

Rules:
1. Start
2. Finish
3. 2 Traps
4. 2 Fortunate Finds
5. 4 Stops Along the Way

STOP

****

The challenge: By what path must I operate in order to be a continuous learner regarding: _____ ?

****

FINISH

START

77. PASS THE TORCH
from Section 5, GAMES FOR CONTINUOUS LEARNING

OBJECTIVE: To use the metaphor of the Olympic torch to help participants identify something specific to teach another person.

PROCEDURE: Draw a picture of the Olympic torch on a whiteboard or flipchart so that all can see it. Use this exercise at the beginning of a meeting on designs for learning. Use it to help individuals see that each person is competent and has much to offer another person. The exercise works best in a group where people know each other, but have not necessarily looked upon each other as teachers and learners. The metaphor of passing the torch will encourage each person. Simply ask the group, What kind of learning can you pass on to your neighbor?   Enliven the group by suggesting that as they think of their own special interest or expertise they raise their hand as if they were holding a torch and passing it on to the next person. Go around the room or table in order, so that each person gets passed to as well as is a passer.

DISCUSSION: If people are slow to get started, give them some clues from the educational or cognitive psychologists. Ask people to look inward to determine if they are good at taking initiative, formulating the right questions, making time for reflection and feedback, rebuilding something after it has fallen apart, explaining, illustrating, analyzing, summarizing, synthesizing, managing projects, drawing conclusions, etc. Try to help people think in terms of their best approaches to problems, not just whether they have specific narrow job skills to share. Learning to learn is a major mandate today, and this goes beyond the narrow content definitions to process definitions.

Benjamin Bloom's taxonomy of objectives in the cognitive domain (1954/ 1980) is still one of the best presentations of learning options for individuals. Peter Senge's concept of "personal mastery" (1990) is similar. Works by both authors are readily available in business and educational libraries.

MATERIALS: Whiteboard or flipchart and marker.

TIME REQUIRED: 30 seconds per person.

78. PERFECT 10s
from Section 5, GAMES FOR CONTINUOUS LEARNING

OBJECTIVE: To borrow the scoring technique from the world of sports to encourage employees to monitor their own progress in learning; to use the self-monitoring scoring technique of gymnastics, diving, or golf to illustrate the technique of continuous monitoring.

PROCEDURE: Use this exercise as an introduction to the idea of continuous learning. Contrast continuous learning with scheduled training classes. Use the exercise at a group or team meeting or in a breakout session at a workshop.

To begin, hand out to each person a copy of the "I CAN DO ONE BETTER!" scorecard (p. 247). Golfers will understand immediately. Those who are not golfers, with a bit of explanation, will too. Most people can relate to either golf, diving, or gymnastics as intensely individual sports in which the player competes vigorously against himself or herself. Generate some energy by asking through show of hands who is or has ever been a golfer, diver, or gymnast, or who has been a close follower of one. Tell the group that players in these sports, especially, have conditioned themselves to continuously monitor their progress. They are individually motivated to better their own scores-- they continuously drive themselves to become better at what they do. Take some time for participants to tell a few stories, if they seem so inclined. Keep the comments focused on the concept of self-monitoring.

By now the group should anticipate what's coming next. Refocus their attention on the " I CAN DO ONE BETTER!" handout. Ask them to substitute their own "sport" (that is, their particular work challenge), and develop a standards matrix for their own learning. Suggest that on the matrix they use words, numbers, symbols, or whatever representation works for them. Start out with just three challenges and three standards to be measured. Later, increase these as people become accustomed to the process of self-monitoring.

Suggest that continuous learning is motivated by continuous measurement. Offer suggestions about types of challenges if people have trouble switching between the creative and the methodical. If folks are having trouble getting started, suggest that they just might be experiencing a lack of mental flexibility-- and that it's this very thing that continuous learning can help to correct.

DISCUSSION: Self-monitoring is a very powerful concept. Being intentional about learning generally increases its power. As people try to articulate their challenges, suggest that they think like the sportsmen and sportswomen in terms of degree of difficulty, pitch and slope, issues of form and timing, and write into their matrices some similar qualifying measures. Suggest that one kind of goal/standard would be a time goal, for example, by day, by week, by month. Another might be a level, such as ability to analyze or evaluate rather than just to accumulate information.

There are many ways to think about one's job and about how to increase one's personal best performance. One simple way to think about perform-ance is to use a "semantic differential" approach which simply suggests that one thinks in terms of ends of a spectrum, such as "Do I want to be more verbal or nonverbal, more rational or intuitive, more realistic or impulsive, etc.?" Another approach is the "people-data-things" job analysis technique used by the Department of Labor in coding jobs. Another is to view perform-ance in terms of the type of "intelligence" it requires, for example, linguistic, spatial, kinesthetic, musical, mathematical, etc. Another is to tie performance to some pre-established standard such as a certification standard. Call on educational and economic research studies if you need them to get folks thinking.

MATERIALS: A "I CAN DO ONE BETTER!" handout for each participant (p. 247).

TIME REQUIRED: About 30 minutes; more if you take the time for stories.

PERFECT 10s

Ellington Ridge Country Club Front Nine
Ellington, Connecticut 1994

HOLE	BLUE	WHITE	RED	PAR	LADIES
1	378	365	350	4	4
2	521	501	441	5	5
3	373	360	274	4	4
4	192	181	167	3	3
5	517	485	445	5	5
6	350	339	325	4	4
7	195	185	159	3	3
8	389	375	285	4	4
9	456	431	398	4	5
OUT	3371	3222	2844	36	37

GOLF COURSE RATING/SLOPE
BLUE 73.9/132
WHITE 71.7/125
RED 70.8/119

I CAN DO ONE BETTER!

Challenges	Goals/Standards		
	high	medium	low
1.			
2.			
3.			

used by permission of Ernest LaRocca, Manager, Ellington Ridge Country Club

247

79. PLAYING IN THE MUD
from Section 5, GAMES FOR CONTINUOUS LEARNING

OBJECTIVE: To critique one's strategic and tactical successes and failures while playing a role-adventure game on the Internet in the "Multi-User Domain (MUD)" for a specified period of time.

PROCEDURE: This exercise is for computer users who are cruisers on the Information Highway. By setting a time limit for play, such as five hours over a period of five days, you'll delimit the time variable so that the strategies of interaction -- with the software, the game program, and the other players-- can be studied. The goal here is to self-study the processes by which one thinks. The design of the self-study is up to each individual.

Ask those who want to play to keep a journal, in any format, about their strategic as well as tactical moves. One way to do this is to create a 2 x 2 matrix, strategic/tactical and success/failure. Another way is to simply write in narrative form what moves were made and why, and what happened as a result of each move. Coding afterward, that is, at the end of each hour or at the end of the exercise, could, in retrospect, identify the successes and failures. After the exercise has been completed by all players, get the players together to discuss their journals.

DISCUSSION: In the MUD, players explore dangerous and exciting territory, spurred on by the pursuit of power, physical prowess, better weapons, stronger magic, etc.-- motivators not unlike many in the fast-moving and changing workplace where, as in a MUD role-play game, a player will make many decisions, both good and bad. Depending on the other process variables, a decision made will have a ripple effect or result in stalemate or even death. Use this exercise as a way to sensitize employees to process variables and to how they think. Help people critique their own capacities to learn from their mistakes. Putting this serious analysis task into the language of a game can help your continuous learners sort out the good from the bad, the productive from the unproductive.

Computer games can be addictive, and this one is especially engaging because of the anonymity and role assumption which characterize play in the MUD. You'll probably never stop computer lovers from playing, so the next best thing to do is to interject a serious purpose to the play. Computer games undoubtedly can stretch our imaginations, and it's this stretch that needs to be captured in self-study in order to re-introduce employees to their creative selves in a purposeful way.

MATERIALS: PCs and Internet connection in the Multi-User Domain; Notebook or paper and pencil for keeping a journal.

TIME REQUIRED: About 10 hours.

80. STORYBOARD TO SUCCESS
from Section 5, GAMES FOR CONTINUOUS LEARNING

OBJECTIVE: To adapt the exercise of creating a storyboard in order to focus a group's thinking on resources they'll need to be continuous learners.

PROCEDURE: Give each person in the group six pieces of plain, unlined paper. Prior to distribution, number each piece of paper so that it can be easily referenced later during discussion. Hold the paper in "landscape" orientation; place the number in the upper right corner, for example, pages numbered 1 - 36 for a group of six persons. These pages will become the "storyboards." Provide identical black felt tip markers for all participants. Provide a stack of extra blank sheets.

Pose questions to the group so that you get specific answers. Do this by asking "What?" and "How?" The questions "When?" "Where?" and "Who?" also lead to specific answers. (Stay away from "Why?"-- save this one for a brainstorming session.) The aim of storyboarding is to get specific answers which lead directly into follow-up action.

Direct participants to write down their responses in as few words as possible, keeping the writing to no more than three items per piece of paper. Suggest that they use a bullet list format or outline form. See example on page 253. Papers will be posted on walls later, and arranged in some kind of order, so all responses must be succinct and easily visible to others. Use masking tape to attach storyboards to the walls.

When all responses have been posted, open discussion and group the storyboards into some logical sets. With another color marker, create a heading for each set. With consensus, discard any duplicate responses. Use the displayed storyboards to lead the group into the next steps of planning.

DISCUSSION: Depending on your time constraints, pose one or more
                  questions for the group to consider.   Here are three
                  possibilities:

        1.   What resources do we need in order to become
                continuous learners as individuals?
        2.   What has to occur in order to shake loose the money
                we need to become a learning organization?
        3.   How should we define "value added" in terms of the
                learning organization?

Many people will find it relatively easy to make connections between the quality movement and the learning organization. These
connections should be encouraged, especially in the areas of
customer service and satisfaction and building quality into products
and processes. If you have had a strong quality thrust to your
operations, by all means build upon what was good in that arena as
you launch into more focused action to bring about continuous
learning.

MATERIALS: Black broad tip markers and a stack of blank numbered
                  storyboards for each participant; several other colored
                  markers; blank sheets of paper; masking tape.

TIME REQUIRED: Variable, depending on group size and number of questions
                  to storyboard; average, about 30 minutes.

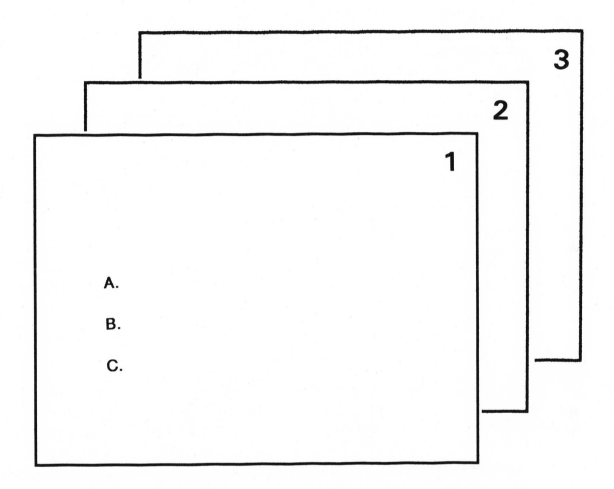

A.

B.

C.

81. SUCCESS IN FAILURE
from Section 5, GAMES FOR CONTINUOUS LEARNING

OBJECTIVE: To use mini case studies of creative risk-taking individuals to help people let go of the inhibiting behaviors that conspire to maintain the status quo.

PROCEDURE: This exercise is a good icebreaker for a team meeting or initial planning session to make a transition into a continuous learning mode of behavior. It works especially well if it can be used upon the heels of a major re-engineering thrust or adoption of a vision statement that spells out a corporate commitment to innovation, creativity, or continuous learning .

Prepare for the meeting by looking through current business magazines (**Forbes**, **Fortune**, **Business Week**, **PC World**, etc.) to find articles about individuals who took risks, made mistakes, and learned from the mistake to ultimately make a major breakthrough for their company. An example is "The Virtue of Making Mistakes" by Brigid McMenamin in **Forbes**, May 9, 1994, pp.192-194. Make copies of these articles to hand out at the meeting. Use several articles on different types of companies; feature both males and females as the risk takers.

Give participants a chance to read through the articles. Don't let them degenerate into a "ha ha" kind of sarcasm that intimates that it's all good words, but that kind of change will never happen around this company! Ask participants to open their minds-- keep the motivation on an up beat. Their job is to keep an open and flexible mindset about the potential for growth in less secure behavior and attitudes. Suggest that they keep these articles in a handy place for reference at any time when things seem to be stuck in a rut.

DISCUSSION: Get the point across that freedom in the workplace means the individual integrity to own one's ideas and work to bring them to fruition under the rule of responsibility. Enterprise, invention, creativity, art, options, modifications,

255

breakthroughs-- all these can follow from learning from one's risky behaviors. Continuous learning is the key.

Career strategists will tell you that it's a good idea to make a list of your successes and your failures before you interview for a new position. Most people don't like to revisit their failures and have not been able to view failure as an old friend. If companies are to ever get out of the "do it right the first time" mentality which always seeks to please the boss, cover the numbers, tell her just what she expects to hear-- individuals will simply have to be able to internalize and articulate their successes in failures. Employees need a lot of help in changing to this kind of honest and flexible mindset. This exercise of mini case studies can help.

MATERIALS: Several case studies from current business magazines. One copy of each article for each participant.

TIME REQUIRED: 10 - 20 minutes.

82. SURGE PROTECTOR
from Section 5, GAMES FOR CONTINUOUS LEARNING

OBJECTIVE: To use the metaphor of a surge protector to help clarify a leader's role in harnessing the energy for moving forward through change.

PROCEDURE: This metaphor is especially relevant to the area of continuous learning. Like the device of the surge protector which grabs ahold of energy and facilitates its useful forward movement, the change leader must grab and direct power surges in the organization so that they can propel a positive change forward and not backwards into destruction. The metaphor is simply a figure of speech which should be used in context as appropriate to motivate and set the tone for discussion and planning which follows. Metaphors can present the big picture of a situation in a very succinct way, thus eliminating the need for much talk at times when too much talking is counterproductive. Use this and other metaphors when the right brain needs prodding and the left brain is tired. Allow the "surge protector" to suggest a new role for leaders.

DISCUSSION: Change brings with it an imbalance in energy, similar to electrical surges due to lightning storms and power outages. Much has been written in recent months about the organizaional need to use that energy to advantage and to not allow it to either dissipate or get wasted on selfish coverups. This is a wake-up call for leadership to take control of the energy that comes with change-- take it early, as a surge protector does on your computer line, and take it forward into new goals and destinations.

A valuable reference regarding change is the little paperback book, **High Velocity Culture Change**, by Pritchett and Pound, Dallas: Pritchett Publishing, 1993. Throughout the book the authors use lively and active metaphors, among them the power surge that accompanies organizational change (p. 10).

MATERIALS :   None.

TIME REQUIRED: 15 - 30 seconds.

257

83. TALENT ON LINE
from Section 5, GAMES FOR CONTINUOUS LEARNING

OBJECTIVE: To create an interactive talent bank on-line in a company's computer network so that expert advice is instantaneously available to any employee who needs it; to empower all employees to seek new learning at the point they need it.

PROCEDURE: Develop a data base system that is user-friendly and which encourages individuals to go on-line with what they consider their unique talent or special skill or understanding. Convey the message to all employees that learning counts and that the more one knows and can share with others who need to know, the better off the entire organization will be. Promote the project of data collection, make it clear that everyone is valued for what he or she has learned and can continue to learn, give employees ample time and motivation to use the system continuously, and make the system fun and easy to use. Tie in suppliers, customers, vendors, board members, and families, if appropriate.

DISCUSSION: Remember that work can be joyous and that computer play is a real turn-on for many people. Learning is infectious; the learner's appetite almost insatiable. Computer technology within companies as well as through the Internet makes asking questions and getting answers the new dialogue of choice at the entry to continuous learning. Figure out a way to capitalize on it in the name of the learning organization!

AT&T, for example, uses an on-line computer service which they call "AAA" (Access to AT&T Analysts) to do just this sort of talent matching. For more information, read the Bennett/ O'Brien article, "The Building Blocks of the Learning Organization," in **Training**, June 1994.

MATERIALS: An on-line system and data base management software.

TIME REQUIRED: Several weeks to set up; seconds per day to use.

84. TIME CAPSULE

from Section 5, GAMES FOR CONTINUOUS LEARNING

OBJECTIVES: To engage in a structured writing exercise about a current corporate event in order to realize the need for flexibility of thinking and expression; to recognize and apply competing motivations and varying assumptions.

PROCEDURE: Do this exercise as part of a workshop or team meeting. It works best around the time of a significant change event-- such as downsizing and resultant organizational restructure, legal action by employees or government agency, bad publicity, internal scandal, announcement of a new benefit plan, etc. Use the upheaval of a specific event to propel the exercise forward.

At the start of the meeting, have the group define the event. This definition will become the title of a "composition" which each participant will write-- in three different versions. Have the group imagine that these writings will be entered in a "Time Capsule" for an imaginary audience to discover 100 years from now as they dig through the artifacts of your corporate civilization to learn about how workplace life was way back then.

Create an actual Time Capsule container in which people can place their finished compositions if you want to be very graphic about the exercise. Later remove them all, make copies of all, and distribute the compositions as a workshop handout memento package for each participant to keep.

The writing task is to write three compositions, all with the same title, but with three different audiences, assumptions, and motivations. The task is to describe the event and its effects on you. Each composition should be no more than 2 pages.

Here are some examples of the variables:
Audience- CEO, CFO, supervisor, spouse, TV news, mother

Assumptions- tell the truth, soften the blow, overinflate, withhold details, fully disclose, expose incompetence

Motivations- hang onto my job, clear my conscience, protect my staff, report the facts, sway public opinion

At the conclusion of writing, ask for several volunteers to read their compositions. Collect all in the Time Capsule, make copies, and later distribute a "book" of them to all participants.

DISCUSSION: The Time Capsule exercise has been around for a long time in training rooms, and it has many variations. This particular version attempts to help participants see that mental flexibility is an important component of learning to learn. This kind of exercise shows people that there isn't just one right answer and that mental dynamism is what's important. Too often, in business as usual, we stop thinking when we've gotten one plausible solution. Continuous learning demands the consideration of multiple solutions and requires intentional flexibility. Competing demands and multiple hypotheses are realities of business life which need to be met head on with flexibility and awareness.

Art Kleiner, in **The Fifth Discipline Fieldbook**, (Currency Doubleday, 1994), writes a section in the chapter on Mental Models called "Writing to Your Loyalties" pp. 268ff. In these pages he describes an exercise related to the Time Capsule exercise. You might find his elaboration and focus of interest too.

MATERIALS: Pencil and paper; a Time Capsule container.

TIME REQUIRED: 30 - 60 minutes.

85. WAR STORIES

from Section 5, GAMES FOR CONTINUOUS LEARNING

OBJECTIVE: To structure a storytelling time as a project debriefing exercise; to engage participants in conscious storytelling as a learning technique.

PROCEDURE: Save this exercise for a project wrap-up or debriefing meeting. Instead of the typical chronological report which generally is given at such a meeting, build in the time and structure for telling stories about the project. Give the project team fair warning, however, so that they refresh their memories about the significant stories about their work. When you announce the wrap-up meeting, tell the group that you expect them to come prepared to tell their own project war stories.

At the meeting, set the stage for storytelling. Arrange chairs in a circle; play soft music; burn incense. Ask one person to be the keeper of the project timeline, and give that person a copy of the project timeline and other relevant activity-focused project documentation in case anyone needs a point of clarification or grounding in the reality of what occurred. Then proceed with the storytelling. Start anywhere, with anyone who has a story to tell about the project. Stories can be silly, deadly serious, cosmic in scope, highly personal, accounts of great skill, or examples of totally missing the mark. They can be funny, sad, outrageous, angry, full of joy.

Continue the storytelling until everyone is satiated with stories. Bring the session to some conclusion with a question such as, "And so what learnings can we take from these stories to our next project and learn again from them?"

DISCUSSION: Storytelling is a form of reporting and communication that has typically been given little space or credence in bureaucratic, accountant-driven workplaces. In workplaces that strive for innovation and added value, customer sensitivity and team building, however, storytelling is recognized as a valuable tool for sharing expertise and insight.   The notion of "war stories" has long been around sales forces. Tales of how the company man or woman overcame great obstacles and hardships in search of a new deal or to squeeze out a few more margin points have been around corporate life for decades. This exercise capitalizes on the memory most people will have of such stories, and legitimizes the process of telling stories as a way to teach and to learn.

With the advent of computer networks and cyberspace chat groups and bulletin boards, storytelling has come out into the open. No longer is it necessary or important that excellent writing style be observed, as in writing memos or letters: on the Internet, people just ask questions and give advice-- tell stories in response to others' knotty problems. Share. Help. Communication has changed; accessibility to information has changed; and formalism has changed. Companies on-line are taking the leap to deliberately build in the time for learning from stories coming across the 'net. Managers and team leaders would do well to exercise the art of storytelling, both on-line and in group meetings. It's an idea whose time has definitely come.

MATERIALS: Stories in people's heads.

TIME REQUIRED: 15 - 60 minutes, depending on the size of the group.

86. WIN WIN

from Section 5, GAMES FOR CONTINUOUS LEARNING

OBJECTIVES: To provide employees with a tool for dealing with conflict; to practice identifying "win win" processes and outcomes as a way to continuously learn.

PROCEDURE: Use this exercise at the beginning of a meeting to focus the group's attention, or as an "energizer" exercise after a break. This mental manipulation is a change in thinking which often results in forward movement through conflict with both aggrieved parties working in parallel for a common good. Learning the technique requires focus, mental flexibility, and a little practice.

Get started by telling the group that, in conflict management, the most important thing is to create a neutral expectation of success for both sides of the conflict. That is, managing conflict requires not that people give up something precious, but that they willingly yield to something new. Both sides of a conflict must be helped to define that newness so that both sides can work to create that something new.

The task of the exercise is to articulate several "new" entities, based either on real current conflicts at work or at home, or on examples of conflicts from anyone's past experience. Give people time to think; then ask for their ideas. If the exercise seems too hard, approach it as a brainstorming exercise and write down all responses, even if they don't seem connected. Enlist the aid of others in the group to bring focus and eventually define some "win win" processes.

DISCUSSION: Help get the group started by suggesting these examples:

1.   Conflict = Husband and wife reading the paper in the living room. Husband opens a window because he's too warm; wife has a cold and is bothered by the draft. ***Setting up the win win:*** open a window in the next room. Husband soon cools off and wife is no longer hit with the blast of cold air. Reading the paper

265

proceeds through the conflict because of the willing yield to something new.

2.   Conflict = The restaurant serves wonderful bread, upon which customers like to pile fresh butter. The cook thinks that the customers' eyes are bigger than their stomachs and refuses to put out crocks of tempting butter because much butter comes back to the kitchen and is wasted. ***Setting up the win win***: wrap the butter in foil in generous individual servings. Customers can still indulge their butter urges and the cook doesn't waste what hasn't been opened. Meals proceed through the conflict situation because of the new entity of generous foil wrapping.

The literature and language of conflict management are full of the notion of "compromise." People hate compromise because it usually implies that each side has to give up something in order for progress to occur. This "win win" technique is an alternative way of thinking about progress that recognizes that the other side never goes away, and that compromise usually fails as a resolution strategy. Working in tandem with the introduction of something new is a far better and more realistic approach to problems.

MATERIALS: None.

TIME REQUIRED: One minute - 20 minutes.

SECTION 6:
GAMES FOR JUST IN TIME TRAINING

GAMES FOR JUST IN TIME TRAINING
Section Overview

Finally, in the drive to ride with change, we acknowledge that most of the competitive improvements that business can make are those which come from the ability of people at work to use the resources at hand. The value added to a business's products and services must come in the creation of quality, user-friendliness, plausible options, timeliness, and other customer sensitive aspects of a worker's output. Each person's ability to learn on the job from the job is the critical skill in human resources development in this era of change.

The skills for job security surely include such things as synthesis, interpretation, acting upon abstract information, discernment, telling the truth, active listening, facilitating, and teaching. All this requires a shift in mindset from group to individual, from classroom to job site. Customized, on the job, investigative, self-initiated, convenient training using technology to support and enhance performance is where the shift is going. Exercises in this final section of **GAMES THAT DRIVE CHANGE** will help you set out in this direction.

87. BAD NEWS, GOOD NEWS
from Section 6, GAMES FOR JUST IN TIME TRAINING

OBJECTIVES: To be intentional about setting up the opportunity to learn, when learning is needed and from whom teaching is desired; to use the dichotomy of "bad news, good news" as a reminder that the two-way process of teaching and learning depends upon both the good and the bad news, upon truth, and upon reflection.

PROCEDURE: "Bad news, good news" is a banner under which to develop new mental models of why and how training should occur. Delivery of just in time training requires first that the employee know what he or she needs to know, and, of course, this means that the "getting stuck" part of the bad news message is often the essence of what drives a person to figuring out what needs to be learned. Use this banner to bring home the message that errors can be your friends, mistakes and wrong turns can yield great insights, experiments that turn out badly can be supremely instructive, and bad news itself must be faced as an opportunity for learning. When companies think and operate only in a good news framework, there is seldom interest in or time for reflection, analysis, and synthesis, all of which must be practiced in today's world of change. It's the bad news that drives the mental processes for this kind of just in time training.

Setting up the training itself can be done in many different ways. Here are some options:
1.   Use internal training consultants on call who work with individuals to find the right training medium and content *(American Greetings did this)*
2.   Create a professional development center geared to individual development through multimedia, video and computer technologies *(American Greetings did this)*
3.   Build in deliberate cross-functional meetings for the sole purpose of learning from each other *(AT&T and Ford did this)*

4. Develop competency standards and goals, and turn people loose to work on achieving them *(Aetna Life & Casualty and FDIC did this)*

5. Be sure that your people have the time for the training they need; build in training time to the regular work day: see it as a value-added component to work

DISCUSSION: One of the hardest things most employees can do is to consistently tell the truth about work results. For a host of cultural reasons, steeped in a history of "Taylorism" (Frederick Taylor (d.1915), work measurement, efficiency, and speed), hampered by persistent "not invented here syndrome," and blinded by an outdated bureaucratic "boss thinks and workers do" mentality, many workers at all levels still act in a way that simply gives the boss what he/she wants to hear. Just in time training breaks this old model. It also depends on telling the truth for its foundation for success.

Facilitating the change in mental models from classroom, mass-production training to immediate needs to know is greatly helped by information technology, including PCs, video, and telephone technologies. Managers, team leaders, and trainers who believe in the basic integrity of individuals to know themselves and want what's best for their own success can be of great assistance to individual learners and of great impact on customer service and retention.

Many vendors are now providing self-paced training hardware, software, programs, and consulting services using multimedia and computer-based instruction of all sorts. Shop around carefully.

MATERIALS: Some "BAD NEWS, GOOD NEWS" slogans on posters, tent cards, bumper stickers-- to put anyplace as a reminder.

TIME REQUIRED: Several seconds to read and digest the message of Bad News, Good News. Various times to set up new just in time training opportunities.

88. BORDER PATROL
from Section 6, GAMES FOR JUST IN TIME TRAINING

OBJECTIVE: To use the analogy and example of an area map to help
               people see that cultural change often occurs at boundaries
               and borders, and that to define the training that's required to
               propel change forward means that individuals must maintain
               watchful "border patrols."

PROCEDURE: Focus a group's thinking on borders by using an overhead
               transparency or handout of an area map-- perhaps the city or
               location in which your business is located. Suggest that, in
               human systems as in the natural world of metallurgy or
               geology, fractures and rifts occur typically at interfaces and
               boundaries.   Point to the areas of the map where
               neighborhoods end and one culture rubs elbows with another
               culture. Ask people for their comments about the
               neighborhoods and what they perceive as the clashes,
               challenges, or disparities at the borders.

               Suggest that the phenomenon of "the border" in commun-
               ities, including work communities, contains within it the
               potential for identifying just in time training that addresses the
               greatest point of acceleration of change.

DISCUSSION: After the group has stretched its thinking about borders, try
               to get them to articulate some of the borders at work. Help
               them to see where corporate or societal changes have
               illuminated the borders-- between departments, functions,
               visions, operational goals, levels of employees, patterns of
               work flow, etc. Help them to identify specific training to meet
               specific challenges at these borders. Facilitate a flipchart
               discussion of just in time training in the context of borders.

One of the great changes that has occurred during the lifetime of readers
of this book is the reshaping of communications by telephone, video, and
computer technologies. The concept of "the global village" is relevant to
discussion of borders or lack of borders and what this means to human
problem solving and harnessing change.

MATERIALS: Area map (transparency or handout); flipchart and marker.

TIME REQUIRED: Several minutes - half an hour.

89. CUT AND PASTE PUZZLE
from Section 6, GAMES FOR JUST IN TIME TRAINING

OBJECTIVE: To play with a puzzle's interchangeable pieces as an analogy
                 for just in time training design ;   to use the puzzle play as an
                 introduction to more efficient and effective instructional
                 design and delivery.

PROCEDURE: Use this puzzle play as an icebreaker or opening exercise at
                 a workshop in instructional design. Copy the puzzle on page
                 277 onto four different colored pieces of paper for each
                 participant. Use index-weight paper if you have it. Provide
                 each person with a set of puzzles and a scissors.   Begin the
                 workshop by having everyone cut the puzzles apart so that
                 there are four pieces of each piece of the puzzle which can be
                 interchanged; that is, any one completed puzzle can be
                 made up of several different colors.

DISCUSSION: Suggest that each of these elements of training could be
                 considered flexible and recyclable from course to course.
                 Get participants thinking in terms of interchangeable parts, of
                 using something from one course in another course in order
                 to save development time and to creatively apply principles
                 from one kind of training to another kind of training. Suggest
                 that participants go one step deeper into the analogy and
                 label some of the colored pieces with actual course titles.
                 Help them to see that some parts can be effectively
                 interchanged; help them to be specific.

                 These are the standard parts of any instructional design effort
                 (add extra pieces if you choose):

                 1.   customer/trainee need
                 2.   topics
                 3.   processes
                 4.   multimedia support and branching
                 5.   case studies/ examples
                 6.   performance criteria and measurement.

Beverly Geber's article "Re-engineering the Training Department" in **Training**, May 1994, pp.27ff., is full of examples and ideas for saving time and increasing effectiveness in training design and delivery. Hewlett-Packard, for example, uses a design template to "repurpose" segments of its courses for just in time training (p. 33); Arthur Andersen consulting company designs courses by a "rapid prototyping" process (p.32f.); and Apple Computer (p. 32) uses a new instructional design expert system to allow almost anyone with ideas to do the rough design of just in time training. The concept of cutting and pasting has been updated with sophisticated computer-based performance support systems. It's well worth your effort to check them out! Read this article first.

MATERIALS: Copies of the puzzle (p. 277) and scissors for each participant.

TIME REQUIRED: 15 minutes.

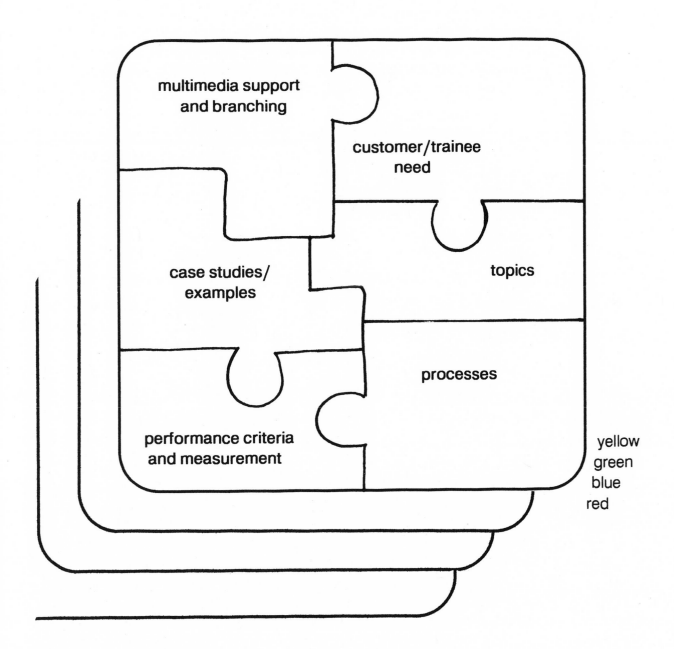

multimedia support
and branching

customer/trainee
need

case studies/
examples

topics

performance criteria
and measurement

processes

yellow
green
blue
red

90. CYBERSPACE HANDSTANDS

from Section 6, GAMES FOR JUST IN TIME TRAINING

OBJECTIVE: To use the image of doing handstands on the Internet as a device to get people to make up new rules for basic communication in cyberspace.

PROCEDURE: Use this as a meeting opener with a group of people who've had experience traveling the Internet. Suggest to them that it's probably about time to develop some "new rules of the ride." Suggest that these new rules will be like doing handstands-- Internet reading, writing, and thinking have turned upside down the traditional ways in which news and ideas have been communicated in our mass culture.

Intentional (that is, efficient, effective, just in time) learning requires that some rules and protocols be observed along the journey. This exercise is a way to begin to develop those rules and behavioral standards as people live through a basic paradigm shift in communication. Record the rules on a flipchart.

DISCUSSION: Take a few minutes to go around the table and ask participants to tell some stories about how they get and give information and about how they've come up against issues of Internet etiquette. After several stories from experienced users, suggest that they try to develop a set of rules for how to communicate on the 'net. Point out ways in which these rules differ from current and past communications rules and behaviors. Suggest that the new rules are necessary in order to keep one's balance; doing "cyberspace handstands" requires awareness and balance.

Time magazine's cover story by Philip Elmer-Dewitt, "Battle for the Soul of the Internet," July 25, 1994, pp.50ff., makes the point that journalism on the Internet is directly opposite traditional journalism, which typically begins at the top with an editor who decides what to publish and reporters who "go and do it." In contrast, on the 'net, news bubbles up from the bottom, unverified, unsanitized, but often closer to the source than anything we've known to date. Understanding such shifts will make better users and better learners.

MATERIALS: Participants' stories; flipchart and marker.

TIME REQUIRED: 5 - 15 minutes.

91. HANDS
from Section 6, GAMES FOR JUST IN TIME TRAINING

OBJECTIVE: To use the symbols of hands to get team leaders or managers to differentiate their roles regarding specific changes.

PROCEDURE: Do this exercise at the beginning of a meeting or workshop session on the need for different management behaviors during times of change. Use it to sensitize leaders about fitting their behavior to tasks at hand-- one size does not fit all during periods of organizational flux. Just in time management is akin to just in time learning. This exercise could be seen as one exercise in "just in time" management training.

Set the stage for discussion by having each participant draw his/her hand (trace one hand with a broad-tip marker) on a flipchart as the group gathers. Draw all hands on the same page-- fill up the page with hands. Use different colors for interest. Hands may be drawn in any position-- fingers spread apart, fingers closed, a hand sideways open or cupped, thumb up, thumb down etc.

On another flipchart, list the following words: strategy, structure, procedure, workflow, acceptance, rewards, systems access, recruitment, communication, learning, direction, coordination, monitoring, evaluation. (Add any others of particular interest to your company.)

DISCUSSION: The ensuing discussion will focus on what changes must be made in each of these areas in order to drive change. The hands will be a reminder that each leader must adopt an attitude regarding his or her involvement: hands on, hands off, hands under, hands around, etc. As each word in the list is discussed, get consensus regarding how leaders should behave regarding that word. Ask the group to call out what they think: that is, "hands on" that issue, "hands around" that one, "hands off" that one, etc. Let discussion flow freely for awhile and then ask for the consensus voice vote regarding what kind of hands are appropriate.

Make the point that different issues during change require different responses. Just in time management in changing times is surely more appropriate than the traditional inflexible recognizable command and control style of the recent past. Just in time management training means differentiating issues and developing an appropriate response for each.

MATERIALS: Two flipcharts and several different colored broad-tip markers.

TIME REQUIRED: 10 - 30 minutes depending on group size.

92. IF I HAD A HAMMER
from Section 6, GAMES FOR JUST IN TIME TRAINING

OBJECTIVE: To use the idea of being a tool for change (a hammer) as a framework for a futuring exercise about training in the new organization.

PROCEDURE: Remind participants of the folksong "If I Had A Hammer" made popular by Pete Seeger and Peter, Paul, and Mary in the '60's. Lead the group in singing, if enough folks remember it:

> If I had a hammer,
> I'd hammer in the morning,
> I'd hammer in the evening,
> All over this land---
> I'd hammer out danger,
> I'd hammer out warning,
> I'd hammer out love between
> My brothers and my sisters,
> All over this land---

The idea is for each participant to use the message of the song as a framework for becoming that hammer, that instrument or tool for action and change. After the song, ask the simple question, "If you had that hammer, what would training/learning look like in the new organization?" Be sure that answers are personal, that is how does _your_ hammer make things happen. Encourage participants to state their descriptions in present tense (disallow use of the terms "will be" and "would be"). Record responses on a flipchart for all to see.

DISCUSSION: The idea contained in the song is the idea of a person in charge of change, activating both the negative and the positive influences on organizational life. Continue the spirit of the song in your discussion by grounding your futuring statements in the reality of the current situation. In classic training needs assessment, this is called the "discrepancy analysis" or starting with the "what is" and moving on to the "what should be." If I had a hammer, I might start at the

283

claw end by ripping out what is currently holding things together-- if I had a hammer, I might build something entirely new upon the remaining foundation of what was yesterday-- if I had a hammer, I'd hammer out warning-- I'd hammer out trust-- I'd hammer out joy in relationships at work-- I'd hammer out truth telling. What would you hammer?

Peter Senge et al.'s **The Fifth Discipline Fieldbook**, New York: Currency Doubleday, 1994, has a very clear section of about ten pages on defining a learning organization (pp. 50 - 59). These pages contain a rather detailed procedure of definition, convergent thinking exercises, divergent thinking exercises, prioritizing, and discussion which any organization could follow in creating its own personalized definition of a learning organization. The experiences of several different organizations are reported. The exercises on these pages are similar in theory to this "If I Had a Hammer" exercise.

MATERIALS: Flipchart and markers.

TIME REQUIRED: 10 - 40 minutes.

93. JUST IN TIME

from Section 6, GAMES FOR JUST IN TIME TRAINING

OBJECTIVES: To create and alter several kinds of training timelines in order to demonstrate how quality can be built into training efforts. To follow Deming's "14 Points" in the revision of the timelines.

PROCEDURE: This can be done as a group or individual exercise. Choose several training projects or opportunities that could be developed as training projects and sketch out a timeline for each one. Choose a different kind of timeline for each project. Here are some examples: flowchart, Gantt chart, calendar, line graph.

Then review Deming's 14 Points. Remove page 287 and place it alongside of your timeline as you consider each point of the timeline. Revise each timeline, point by point. Scanning back and forth between the 14 Points and the timeline, push back the decision points on the timeline or make modifications that will result in building quality into the training process.

DISCUSSION: By reviewing each point in the timelines according to the 14 Points, you should be able to significantly revise your training development and implementation processes to make them not only more efficient, more appropriate, more just in time, but also of higher quality. W. Edwards Deming spent a lifetime preaching and practicing the gospel of building quality in (not inspecting it out). Just in time training design is one of the ways his followers adapt the 14 Points.

Of Deming's 14 Points, these six are perhaps the most relevant to revision of training timelines: 5, Improve constantly the system of production and service; 6, Institute training on the job; 9, Break down barriers between departments; 12, Remove barriers that rob workers, engineers, and managers of their right to pride of workmanship; 13, Institute a vigorous program of education and self-improvement; and 14, Put everyone to work to accomplish the transformation. Deming's unique contribution was to advocate that quality is everyone's job. Learning is everyone's job too.

MATERIALS: Your own constructed training timelines and page 287.

TIME REQUIRED: 30 - 60 minutes, depending on the number of timelines.

DEMING'S 14 POINTS
for building quality in

1. Create constancy of purpose.
2. Adopt the new philosophy.
3. Cease dependence on mass inspection to achieve quality.
4. End the practice of awarding business on price tag alone. Instead, minimize total cost, often accomplished by working with a single supplier.
5. Improve constantly the system of production and service.
6. Institute training on the job.
7. Institute leadership.
8. Drive out fear.
9. Break down barriers between departments.
10. Eliminate slogans, exhortations, and numerical targets.
11. Eliminate work standards (quotas) and management by objective.
12. Remove barriers that rob workers, engineers, and managers of their right to pride of workmanship.
13. Institute a vigorous program of education and self-improvement.
14. Put everyone in the company to work to accomplish the transformation.

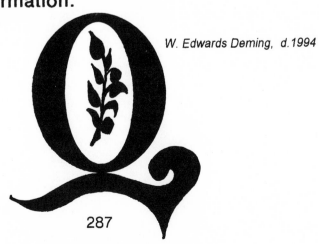

W. Edwards Deming, d.1994

94. ON A SCALE OF 1 TO 10...

from Section 6, GAMES FOR JUST IN TIME TRAINING

OBJECTIVE: To vote with your feet on a scale of 1 to 10 on training readiness, as a dramatic way of indicating need for just in time training.

PROCEDURE: Before developing a "course" for classroom delivery, find out exactly who needs it. Do this by gathering a group of potential students together and ask them to vote by standing next to a number representing a scale of 1 to 10, number 1 being low and number 10 being high. Before the group assembles, place colored paper with large numbers around the room, one number per piece of paper. Participants on cue will stand beside the number which most represents their own individual "current knowledge" of the topic at hand.

DISCUSSION: After the voting, you will probably find a rather unevenly distributed group of scores, indicating some people are more knowledgeable than others, and therefore not in as much need for the training you had in mind. This exercise is a reality check against over-zealous training developers, managers, and instructors who often think that they know best and who consequently waste a lot of time in designing training for many folks who simply don't need it. Save training for the right people at the right time. It's their sense of timing and need that matters, not yours.

> This exercise is akin to pre- and post-testing evaluation along a scale of numbers. If you conduct scale-based voting of any kind, remember to have a scale of at least 5 points; 7 points is even better; and a scale of 1 to 10 is familiar and comfortable for most folks. Being able to refer back to frequency counts and scale numbers helps people anchor their ideas onto something tangible.

MATERIALS: Colored paper with a number (1 to 10) on each piece.

TIME REQUIRED: 3 minutes.

95. Q-SORT

from Section 6, GAMES FOR JUST IN TIME TRAINING

OBJECTIVES: To use the Q-Sort data collection methodology to design just in time training for a newly merged, downsized, or drastically changed business; to lead a training organization in creating new kinds of training to fit a new company.

PROCEDURE: This is an exercise that works well in a small training department (3 - 6 persons). It can be effectively used with benchmarking information.

First, develop a sample of many kinds of possibilities for training in the new organizations of your company. Use benchmarking information collected from other companies, use magazine and newspaper articles about good ideas or trends, use your own course catalogs, make up "stretch" potentials, use competitor information, use supplier and customer information, etc. Think in terms of all kinds of training: classroom, CBT, video, take-home training, one to one peer training, team training, cross-functional training, customer training, etc.   The object is to create a card deck made up of all these possibilities for training.

Write one suggestion on each card. Use 4 x 6 index cards. Place a number on each card for easy reference later. This become the "Q-Deck." The Q-Deck is then sorted by each participant in turn.   Sorting can be done in private and the order recorded by each participant, for discussion later at a group meeting.

Develop a rating form to be filled out by each participant. Ask participants to complete the form after their sort. Each card should be rated on a scale of 1 to 7, going from "dislike" to "like" or "least like my view" to "most like my view." Numbers of the cards are listed down the left side of the form, something like this: *Dislike*   *Like*

1.

2.

3.

As participants begin to sort the deck, suggest that they first do a rough sort into "agree," "neutral," and "disagree" piles, then later do the final rating on the 7-point scale.

DISCUSSION: Q-Sort is a systematic way of understanding subjective opinion. Because opinion is collected and recorded individually, the data collection and interpretation is as valid as possible from that individual's unique perspective.

When the participants come together for group discussion of their ratings, ask for explanations of the ratings. The smaller the group, the deeper the discussion can be. Take the discussion as far as possible by including other questions such as, How do you think the CEO would sort the cards? How would you sort the cards 5 years from now? How would our top three customers like to see the cards sorted? Continue discussion as long as it is productive.

Q-Sort methodology has been fostered by The International Society for the Scientific Study of Subjectivity located at the University of Missouri at Columbia. Analysis and interpretation of results can be enhanced by factor analysis for in-depth understanding of the psychological and statistical bases of subjective ratings.

MATERIALS: The Q-Sort card deck of samples and a rating form for each participant. Flipchart and markers for group discussion later.

TIME REQUIRED: 30 - 60 minutes of individual sorting and rating per participant; 1 hour for group discussion.

96. RETURN TO SENDER
from Section 6, GAMES FOR JUST IN TIME TRAINING

OBJECTIVE: To write yourself a letter stating exactly how you can further the cause of becoming a learning organization through specific kinds of just in time training that you yourself initiate over the next 3 months; to then place the letter in an envelope to be mailed back to you at the end of the specified 3-month period.

PROCEDURE: Do this game at the start of making changes toward an organization's becoming a learning organization. At a team or group meeting, ask participants to write down at least three specific training items which they will initiate in order to become better performers on their jobs. Set a time limit for accomplishing these things, such as 3 months. Hand out brightly colored paper and envelopes. Use several different colors of paper and envelopes-- hot pink, sunshine yellow, bright green, hot turquoise.

Ask participants to address the envelope to themselves at their home addresses, place the letter in the envelope, and seal it. All sealed, addressed envelopes should then be placed in a large clear glass brandy snifter or punch bowl in a reception area, near the copy machine, or in the manager's or team leader's office -- in some highly visible place as a reminder to all of their commitments.

At the end of the 3-month period, ask a secretary to mail each envelope back to the person who wrote the letter.

DISCUSSION: After the letters have been received and reviewed by the originators, call a meeting of all participants to talk about the reality of what they were actually able to do during the 3-month period. Focus on what was the ideal and what is the reality. Identify problems, roadblocks, and obstacles to success. Seek ideas from the group about how to prevent or overcome these problems in order to truly become self-propelled individual learners and a learning organization.

This game is adapted from one used by the congregation at Jeffersonville Presbyterian Church, Jeffersonville, Pennsylvania. Their version of it asks participants to write down how each person "can make a difference" during the specified period, in their case, one year. At the end of the year, all letters are returned to the sender for reflection. Thanks to Pearl Detwiler, Circle Leader, at the church.

MATERIALS: Colored envelopes and stationery; postage for mailing.

TIME REQUIRED: 10 - 20 minutes.

97. 7 SHADES OF GRAY

from Section 6, GAMES FOR JUST IN TIME TRAINING

OBJECTIVE: To do a self-referenced, just in time, training needs assessment based on new business paradigms of what's important for survival and success at the uncertain dawn of the new century.

PROCEDURE: Design a 10 - 20 item list of elements of "the new paradigms" which seem to be important in your particular company. Beside each item present a 7-point rating scale so that each participant can rate himself/herself on each. Have each participant place a large dot or an X on the line opposite each item. Connect the dots (Xs) in a profile for later display of all participants' profiles. The assembled profiles will give you a quick glance at your workforce's need for critical training to meet the changing times.

Here are some item suggestions and an idea of what the rating form might look like:

	small need						**great need**
1. Information services	|	|	|	|	|	|	|
2. Advanced skill in current job	|	|	|	|	|	|	|
3. Cross-functional skills	|	|	|	|	|	|	|
4. Impact of global competition	|	|	|	|	|	|	|
5. Innovation	|	|	|	|	|	|	|
6. Performance measurement	|	|	|	|	|	|	|
7. Contribution to measurement quality	|	|	|	|	|	|	|
8. Productivity measurement	|	|	|	|	|	|	|
9. New systems and organizational relationships	|	|	|	|	|	|	|

The question for each person to ask himself/herself is this:

"What need for just in time training do I personally have in each of these areas of 'new paradigm'?"

DISCUSSION: Many observers of the current business scene comment that there is no convenient model for organizational effectiveness. If there's any agreement at all, it seems to be that individuals must increasingly take responsibility for their own advancement, their own learning, and their own specific training. Time is compressed at all levels of organization, and the need for just in time interventions of all sorts seems to be great. Helping individuals be effective self-assessors is an important function for human resources professionals, especially for training specialists. This exercise can help.

There are many mixed signals today for individuals at work. The push for quality often seems at dissonance with the need to improve productivity, the emphasis on teamwork often seems at odds with the need to look out for #1 as downsizing and efficiencies in operations proliferate. Helping employees improve themselves and the organization through learning and training are tangible ways to foster integrity in a sea of contradictions.

MATERIALS: A list of important "new paradigm" items in your company and a rating scale for each participant.

TIME REQUIRED: 5 - 15 minutes to do the rating; as much time as you need for group discussion and profile comparison.

98. THIS TO THAT

from Section 6, GAMES FOR JUST IN TIME TRAINING

OBJECTIVE: To do a "matching" exercise from mixed-up sets of words representing the old way and the new way in workplace training.

PROCEDURE: Use this at the beginning of a group meeting. It's a takeoff on the kids' game of connecting the pairs of words. It makes a good focusing exercise at the beginning of a training organization meeting or training design session.

Distribute a copy of the word list "This to That" (page 299) to each participant. Instruct them to draw a line connecting each pair of words-- one from the "This" column connected to one from the "That" column. Here's an example:

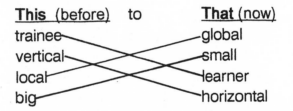

When everyone seems to have finished, do a quick verbal check of the tough ones to be sure everyone has gotten them connected correctly. Then go on to the business of training design for the new look around your company.

DISCUSSION: People have been hearing the new "good words" often-- in the press, on TV, in business magazines and journals, at professional association conferences, and even probably at work through vision statements and company publications. However, making the new good words work in the reality of re-designed training and new organizational relationships is still difficult. Exercises like this help employees to internalize the good words and use them to focus on the tough job ahead of planning and implementing change.

A more active variation of this exercise is to present the lists unscrambled. The "This" list is on one side of the room and the "That" list is on the other side of the room. Participants line up as in a spelling bee. When the word pairs are called out by a leader (e.g., trainee--learner) each person in turn moves to the word with which he or she feels most comfortable. This exercise shows you in a dramatic way where you must do the most work in terms of changing people's attitudes and directions. It makes a good "energizer" exercise after a break or lunch.

MATERIALS: Word lists (page 299) and pencils for each participant.

TIME REQUIRED: 5 - 10 minutes.

THIS TO THAT

THIS (before)

THAT (now)

	THIS (before)	THAT (now)
1.	trainee	global
2.	vertical	small
3.	local	learner
4.	big	horizontal
5.	classroom training	empowerment
6.	off-site seminars	on the job training
7.	incremental change	speak up
8.	control	collaborate
9.	keep quiet	revolutionary change
10.	dictate	individual training
11.	play it safe	ask for help
12.	do it yourself	go for it
13.	wait	take risks

Note: Add other word pairs that are of special importance to your organization.

99. WE AND I

from Section 6, GAMES FOR JUST IN TIME TRAINING

OBJECTIVE: To use the Malcolm Baldrige National Quality Award 1995 criteria in "Employee Education, Training, and Development (section 4.3)" as a guideline for your group's definition of types of training which they now need.

PROCEDURE: Write the terms listed below from the 1995 Baldrige National Quality Award <u>Award Criteria</u> booklet (p.28) on a flipchart or overhead transparency so the whole group can see it. Ask each participant to place the numbers of the items down the left margin of a piece of paper and make 2 columns on the paper, one entitled "I" and the other entitled "We." As you read each term from the list, participants record a tic mark in the appropriate "I" or "We" column. That is, each participant must decide whether he or she needs training in that particular item (the "I" column) as well as decide whether the group needs training in that particular item too (the "We" column). After the individual assessments, call for a show of hands from the group as you read each item again. The time frame is now, not what is needed 3 months or 6 months from now. Here's the list:

		I	**We**
1.	leadership skills		
2.	communications		
3.	teamwork		
4.	problem solving		
5.	interpreting and using data		
6.	meeting customer requirements		
7.	process analysis		
8.	process simplification		
9.	waste reduction		
10.	cycle time reduction		
11.	error-proofing		
12.	priority setting based on cost/benefit data		
13.	basic skills (literacy and basic math)		
14.	safety		
15.	customer contact training		

301

DISCUSSION: After the individual voting, hold a general discussion on the
                15 points. Pay special attention to those areas in which
                individuals indicated they personally need training now-- and
                get on with the training design and development. Also spend
                some time talking about the group's concept of "We" -- get
                them used to thinking very personally (that is, in the first
                person singular and plural) as you re-design training for the
                new world. Gone are the days of third party-- "he/she did it
                to me; they ran the training." It's all up close and personal in
                the new world of rapid change.

If you're not on the mailing list to receive updated versions of the
Malcolm Baldrige Award Criteria, write to the American Society for
Quality Control, P.O. Box 3005, Milwaukee, WI 53201-3005 and
request to be placed on the list. There's no charge, and it's a great
way to keep up to date.

MATERIALS: A list of terms from the Baldrige Award Criteria, pencil and
                paper for each participant, flipchart and marker or overhead
                transparency and projector.

TIME REQUIRED: 10 - 20 minutes.

100. WHO'S WHO

from Section 6, GAMES FOR JUST IN TIME TRAINING

OBJECTIVE: To create an on-line directory of personal resources, updated at specific points, for all to read-- an accessible "Who's Who" of talent that can be tapped by anyone at anytime for learning.

PROCEDURE: Focus on specialized job skills as well as related beyond-the-job skills. That is, have two sections to the entry, both of which can be of use to others as you seek to become a learning organization. Encourage participants to list the things they like to do and can do well, even if they are not presently doing them on the job. Such job-related skills might include: writing, graphics, navigating the Internet, or job-specific skills like closing a sale, success at cold calling, speed arithmetic, organizing files, creating computer spreadsheets, etc. Beyond-the-job skills might include such things as: square dancing, cross-country skiing, surfing, figure skating, coaching basketball, aerobic instruction, nutrition counseling, teaching CPR, etc.

Create a section of the on-line entry form for participants to list "potential learning opportunities"-- perhaps a space for up to five ideas for conferences, workshops, CBT, video, multimedia, peer training, or individual improvement ideas. You'd be surprised at how people will talk to their computers more readily than they will speak up in meetings.

The key to this "Who's Who" is for it to be accessible to all at all times for read-only. At appointed times during the year, for example, once every quarter, all files will be updated by the originator. Create a "Who's Who" directory with individual files of persons. Cross-reference and make it as sophisticated as you want to as the system gets used.

DISCUSSION: In old-style business environments, training tended to be designed by "others" -- and fielded and promoted through course catalogs and brochures enticing folks to come. Often, this kind of training missed the target for most trainees, and it was not immediately useful. Training support for performance was certainly not just-in-time, and that time lag resulted in time wasted and resources lost. In this old style, top-down training, participants tended not to share with each other what _they_ knew or demonstrate the skills which they had.

In the new style training, however, all this changes. New style training is bottom-up, that is, individually based, skill based, and performance based. New style training is just in time and collaborative. It depends on empowered individuals-- all persons at work-- and it is the foundation for continuous learning.

```
+---------------------------------------------------+
|                          originator identification:|
|                          _____|
|  Job related skills:                               |
|    1                                               |
|    2                                               |
|    3                                               |
|    4                                               |
|    5                                               |
|  Beyond the job skills:                            |
|    1                                               |
|    2                                               |
|    3                                               |
|    4                                               |
|    5                                               |
|  Potential learning opportunities:                 |
|    1                                               |
|    2                                               |
|    3                                               |
|    4                                               |
|    5                                               |
|                                                   |
+---------------------------------------------------+
```

MATERIALS: An on-line "Who's Who" data entry format, similar to the one above.

TIME REQUIRED: 15 - 30 minutes for data entry and periodic access.

304

INDEX

ABOUT THE AUTHOR

Carolyn Nilson is a training consultant to many of the world's most successful, prestigious, and forward-looking corporations. These include: The ARINC Companies, AT&T, Chemical Bank, Chevron, Martin Marietta, Nabisco, and The World Bank. Dr. Nilson has also consulted with government agencies: the National Institute of Education, the US Department of Education, the US Department of Labor, and state departments of education. She has recently been a speaker at national conferences of the American Society for Training and Development (ASTD), American Management Association, and National Society for Performance and Instruction. She has been a faculty member at Padgett-Thompson, the Ziff Institute, and the US Armed Services Training Institute. A former training executive, she held management positions in state-of-the-art applications at AT&T Bell Laboratories and Combustion Engineering. Dr. Nilson's work has been featured in recent editions of business magazines: *Successful Meetings*, *Training*, *Training & Development*, *Entrepreneur*, and *Fortune*. Her books have been chosen by MacMillan's Executive Program Book Club and Business Week Book Club, and have been reviewed by ASTD and featured in ASTD's publications. She is the author of eight previous training books, among them the popular *TEAM GAMES FOR TRAINERS* published by McGraw-Hill.